Wade Akins' life reads like an adventure nove[...]tures, and ministries with the spirit of a true p[...]sionate or creative individual. He lives and br[...]Gospel. He longs to see new converts experie[...] in their lives. This is a man who has been there and done that! Revival just seems to happen when he ministers. God is there. Christ is honored. You must read these pages.

James T. Draper, President
LifeWay Christian Resources

Wade Akins has demonstrated consistently across the years the truths about which he writes in this book on the Lordship of Christ. Probably no single international figure has been more greatly used of God to bring people to Christ than Wade Akins. The secret of his success will become apparent in the pages of *Be a 24/7 Christian*. Jesus is Lord of his life. Consequently, he has enjoyed the blessings of the power of God. Read it, contemplate it, and the results in your own life will not be dissimilar.

Paige Patterson, President
Southwestern Baptist Theological Seminary

You will want the words written on the tombstone of Sherry (Akins) to be written on yours: "The purpose of my life is to glorify Christ both in my life and in my death." Read this book by my dear brother and good friend, Wade Akins, and follow the path revealed in its pages to His Lordship crowned over your life.

Gordon Fort, Vice President for Overseas Operations
International Mission Board, Southern Baptist Convention

From the jungles of Vietnam and Brazil and through the cities of North America, missionary strategist, evangelist, and church planter Wade Akins vividly recounts a thrilling life of adventure and passionately relates the spiritual lessons learned from a life lived under the Lordship of Christ. *Be a 24/7 Christian* is a must read for anyone interested in missions and evangelism in the 21st Century.

Robin Hadaway, Associate Professor of Missions
Midwestern Baptist Theological Seminary
Former Regional Leader, Eastern South America
International Mission Board, Southern Baptist Convention

Wade is a man who is totally committed to doing the will of God wherever His Lord leads him. You will be encouraged to read a book that will give practical help from a man who has positioned himself to allow Christ to be Lord of every area of His life.

Johnny Hunt, Senior Pastor
First Baptist Church
Woodstock, Georgia

Wade Akins has demonstrated, in a million ways and in a hundred countries and through an untold number of languages, the Lordship of Christ. I have witnessed his walk through the valley of death, atop the roof of a van preaching, and in a multitude of other settings throughout his soul-winning, missionary life! This book is a personal encounter with a 24/7 Christian under the Lordship of Christ!

Bobby Welch, Senior Pastor
First Baptist Church
Daytona Beach, Florida
President, Southern Baptist Convention

Wade Akins is a man who walks his walk and talks his talk. Better said, the tongue in his shoe and the tongue in his mouth go in the same direction. While some debate about Lordship salvation, Wade is a pragmatist who believes whatever you call it, the result will be the same . . . Evangelism and Missions. He cuts through the definition of *Lordship* to the description of it. *Be a 24/7 Christian* is a must for every growing disciple who burns with the desire to crown Jesus Christ Lord of every area of his or her love, loyalty, and life. Without reservation I recommend Wade Akins and his book to you.

Ken Whitten, Senior Pastor
Idlewild Baptist Church
Tampa, Florida

Rarely does someone have anything truly profound to say. But Wade Akins has proven to be among those who are indeed rare. He blends first-hand experiences with objective, spiritual principles to generate a blueprint for life itself, all centered around the Lordship of Christ!

Keith Eitel, Chairman
Missions Department
Southeastern Baptist Theological Seminary

Living the adventure of submission to Jesus as Lord is Wade Akins' life message. After reading *Be a 24/7 Christian*, you will want to make it yours as well.

Jeff Iorg, President
Golden Gate Baptist Theological Seminary

Those who desire to develop a deeper relationship with God would do well to read Wade Akins' book. His own journey will inspire and instruct yours.

Mark Terry, A. P. Stone Professor of Missions and Evangelism
Southern Baptist Theological Seminary

Wade Akins has a passion to see people saved and to experience the joy of living under the Lordship of Jesus Christ. *Be a 24/7 Christian* gives eloquent testimony of this passion. You will especially enjoy the personal stories of transformed lives that this faithful missionary shares throughout.

Daniel L. Akin, President
Southeastern Baptist Theological Seminary

I have known Wade Akins for several years and have had the privilege of serving with him on the mission field on several occasions. My life has not been the same since. He is the real deal. His life is the Christ-life with a purpose that is clear, concise, and compelling. If you desire to grow closer to Christ and impact the Kingdom of God, reading *Be a 24/7 Christian* is a must!

Mark Anderson, Senior Pastor
Colonial Heights Baptist Church
Jackson, Mississippi

Wade Akins has lived life under the Lordship of Jesus Christ! His journey has been filled with encounters with God that have been life-changing for him and for those around him. What he has done in the pages of this book is to capture the theological, practical, and applicable principles of living a life that honors Jesus as Lord. These pages allow the reader to peer through the window of a man's soul to discover the secret of what it means when a man has a relationship with God. The stories are clear, the Scriptures are relevant, and the reading is captivating. Wade Akins has provided a practical guide for any Christian to understand the concept of the Lordship of Christ for daily living.

Nick Garland, Senior Pastor
First Baptist Church
Broken Arrow, Oklahoma

Wade Akins has written a book that clearly defines and illustrates Lordship. Every serious believer should read it.

Ted Kersh, Pastor
First Baptist Church
Claremore, Oklahoma

From the piney woods of north Louisiana to the steamy rain forests of Brazil, Wade Akins has followed Jesus Christ. Decades ago He made Jesus Lord of his life. He has followed Our Lord around the world spreading the Gospel. These stories will bless you, inspire you, and sometimes bring you to tears. In *Be a 24/7 Christian* he will tell you how to make Jesus Lord of your life.

Paul Brooks, Senior Pastor
First Baptist Church
Raytown, Missouri

Wade Akins does more than write about the importance of the Lordship of Christ. He illustrates it with powerful stories of men and women who live out this principle on a daily basis. Give yourself plenty of time to settle down with this book and let its truths settle down in you.

Tom Elliff, Senior Pastor
First Baptist Church
Del City, Oklahoma
Former President, Southern Baptist Convention

In all of my years I have never met anyone who has lived under the Lordship of Christ like my dear friend, Wade Akins. Read this modern-day apostle Paul. Your life will never be the same!

James Merritt, Senior Pastor
Cross Pointe—The Church at Gwilcott Corner
Greater Atlanta, Georgia
Former President, Southern Baptist Convention

I am Wade's pastor and have been a close friend for over 25 years. A quote in the book says, "Whatever you are surrendered to defines your life." Wade is defined by the Lordship of Jesus Christ. *Be a 24/7 Christian* is an expression of how one comes under the Lordship of Christ and how one lives and dies under the Lordship of Christ. It is a must read for every believer who desires to be salt and light in a tasteless and dark world. It's a must-read for nonbelievers, for it will draw them to Jesus.

Philip D. Jett, Senior Pastor
Englewood Baptist Church
Jackson, Tennessee

This is an excellent work to inspire mature believers, strengthen new Christians, and communicate the gospel to those who have not yet received the Lord. Wade's personal experiences illustrate the biblical truths masterfully.

Emil Tuner, Executive Secretary
Arkansas Baptist Convention

Wade Akins, like no one else I know, is the Apostle Paul of our age. His life and ministry are one of dramatic results—seeing countless numbers of people trust Christ and many more empowered to tell others about Jesus. *Be a 24/7 Christian* is not only an opportunity to be enthralled with the exciting story of the spread of God's church throughout the world but to see the life of a man who is living on the cutting edge of God's Kingdom.

Chuck McAlister, Senior Pastor
Second Baptist Church
Hot Springs, Arkansas

The Church needs *Be a 24/7 Christian*. We need to be reminded of the truths Wade emphasizes. He is Lord! and we must live it! This is a supplement to the supreme Book on Lordship. How we need to follow the guidelines of both! This really reaches my soul and satisfies a need to hear the truths once more put so succinctly.

Diane Reeder, Member
Board of Trustees
International Mission Board

I have been privileged to follow God's work through Wade in the war-torn country of Vietnam; the streets of Washington, D.C.; the towns, cities, and villages of Brazil; and now around the world. The stories he relates will challenge you to a fresh yielding of your life to His Lordship.

Wayne Jenkins, Director of Evangelism
Louisiana Baptist Convention

Little attention is being given in our churches to nurturing believers to a deeper walk with the Lord and a fully surrendered life. Wade Akins' delightful narrative format highlights the basic teachings of Scripture regarding the Christian life. The reader can identify with many of the experiences common to each of us and will stand in awe at others as Wade relates incidents on the mission field which reveal God's power and demonstrate His faithfulness. This book will be an inspirational renewal for all who read it and a challenge to go all the way with Christ.

Jerry Rankin, President
International Mission Board, SBC

Wade Akins may be one of our greatest living missionaries. His life of living under Christ's Lordship has resulted in hundreds and hundreds of churches planted and thousands of people brought into the Kingdom. The acid-test of Lordship is that God's Kingdom is advanced through our lives. *Be a 24/7 Christian* tells how that can happen by one who has lived it out.

Bill Eliff, Senior Pastor
Summit Church
Little Rock, Arkansas

Exciting. Biblical. Practical. Those words only begin to describe *Be a 24/7 Christian*. This isn't simply a theological treatise on a great doctrine of the Bible. Wade's life experiences illustrate the great truths presented. His pointed questions will probe the deep parts of your heart. His practical insights will enable you to do that which God has called you to do—allow Jesus full control of your life. You'll laugh, then cry. But in the end, you'll find yourself bowing before Jesus and crowning Him as Lord.

Sammy Tippit
International Evangelist

If C.S. Lewis was the most thoroughly converted man I know of, Wade Akins is the most thoroughly committed man I know. He has a one-track mind that runs straight to Jesus. *Be a 24/7 Christian* is packed with spiritual truth drawn from the life experiences of a unique man of God I have lived with, prayed with, worked with, cried with, and rejoiced with for more than 40 years.

Dr. Cecil R. Taylor
Dean of the Department of Religion
University of Mobile, Alabama

As Wade Akins writes with transparent honesty about his spiritual journey around the world, he makes applications that point the way to living the life that counts now and forever. Absorb these stories and their lessons, and then be quick to share them with as many people as possible.

Wayne Bristow
International Evangelist

Wade Akins' newest book breathes with both passion and practicality. It is eminently useful to the believer who longs to "put feet to faith." This is no theory for endless debate; it is a manual for warfare at a time when the army of our King requires soldiers who will lay down their lives for the sake of His name.

Stan May, Chairman
Missions Department
Mid-America Baptist Theological Seminary

CHRISTIAN

WADE AKINS

HANNIBAL BOOKS
www.hannibalbooks.com

To Barbara

my wonderful wife.
She is my "God's gift of grace."
She not only is my loving wife, she also ministers
with me around the world and has been
a strong support and help
as I wrote this book.

Barbara is a very special person
to me and to all who know her personally.

To order more copies of
Be A 24/7 Christian

Contact:
Hannibal Books
P.O. Box 461592
Garland, Texas 75046-1592

Fax: 1-972-487-7960
Phone: 1-800-747-0738 or 972-487-5710
Email: hannibalbooks@earthlink.net
Visit: www.hannibalbooks.com

Order form in back of this book.

Acknowledgements

Special thanks to:
- My dad and mom, Vernon and Marjorie Akins, who reared me in a Christian and loving family.
- My sister, Katherine, who has been a loving friend.
- My wonderful three children—Christy, Timothy, and Jason—who love me and support me more than words can express.
- Wayne Bristow, international evangelist, who encouraged me to write the stories and this book and who worked diligently in polishing every story. Without Wayne this book would not have been written.
- Dr. Danny Akin, president of Southeastern Baptist Theological Seminary, who read the manuscript to assure theological correctness.
- Dr. Ray P. Rust, who taught me and discipled me when I was a teen-ager.
- Dr. Cal R. Guy, who taught me in missions and was used of God to open my heart for the call to go to the foreign mission field.
- Walter A. Routh, former missionary in South Vietnam, who mentored me on the mission field.
- David Wilson, president of Open Air Campaigners, who taught me to how preach on the streets effectively using the special "paint-talk" method.
- Dr. Waylon Moore, who taught me discipleship and to be incarnational in ministry.
- Special friends such as international evangelist Sammy Tippit; Dr. Paul Brooks, pastor of First Baptist Church, Raytown, MO.; Dr. Cecil Taylor, dean of religion at Mobile University; Rev. David Orr, pastor of the Weems Creek Baptist Church in Annapolis, MD., and Dr. Phil Jett, my dear

friend and pastor of the Englewood Baptist Church in Jackson, TN, and many other friends whom I cannot name in this acknowledgement, for the list would be too long.

• Gary and Lisa Taylor of Gary Taylor Investments. Gary is a close and dear friend and has walked "with" me through the toughest trials of my life.

I especially want to thank Jesus Christ for giving me a new life.

In memory of

SHERRY DEAKINS AKINS, my wife for 23 years, who lived her life under the Lordship of Christ. Sherry died on the foreign mission field on December 4, 1993, inside the will of God. She said, "The purpose of my life is to glorify Christ in both my life and in my death." That says it all.

JOE FRANK AKINS, my brother, who committed his life to the Lordship of Christ and became mightily used of God to win young people to Christ. He and his wife, Doliene, began Grace Christian Homes in Shreveport, Louisiana. and ministered to troubled teens from all over America. He died of cancer in February 2003.

Contents

I. Significance of Lordship   19
   1. The Book   20
   2. Living to What End?   22
   3. The Promise   25
   4. The Chess Game   28
   5. Standing in the Gap   33
II. Surrender to Lordship   37
   6. The Trail   38
   7. "Kill Me"   43
   8. "I Love You. I Love You. I Love You."   55
III. Struggling with Lordship   63
   9. The Lion Within   64
   10. On the Roof Tops   71
   11. Struggles We Face   80
   12. Lessons from the Practice Field   91
   13. A Work in Progress   97
   14. The End of the Story   107
IV. Secret of Lordship   115
   15. The Ring   116
   16. How to Stop a Truck   126
   17. Listen. God is Saying Something   132
V. Serving Under Lordship   143
   18. A Captive Audience   144
   19. Extraordinary Encounters   148
   20. Love Without Borders   155
   21. Amazing Grace   162

Foreword

Wade Akins is one of a kind. When God made him, He "broke the mold." I stand in awe of his vision, his courage, his abounding energy, and his incredible focus.

Everywhere Wade Akins goes, revival seems to break out and evangelism follows. Why is this? The answer may be found in the subject of this book—the lordship of Jesus Christ.

Wade Akins seems to have a total abandonment to the concept of the lordship of Jesus Christ. I have noticed that when a person is abandoned to Jesus, Jesus, likewise, gives Himself to that person in incredible power. God is looking for people to whom and through whom He can show Himself powerful. Wade seems to be that kind of a person.

No greater cause exists than to bring people bound in the golden chains of the Gospel, teach them to say that Jesus is Lord, and lay them at Jesus' feet. That's what this book is about.

As you read, you are not reading the musings of an armchair philosopher. Nor are you reading the imaginative events of an emotionalist. You are reading events that read like an additional chapter to the Book of Acts.

Events like this help to confirm our faith and stir us on to missions and evangelism, because what God does through one, He can do through another. God has intimates, but He does not have favorites. Anybody who wants in on the action can do it.

I trust that God will use what you are about to read to soften your heart, illumine your mind, and put steel in your backbone.

Adrian Rogers, Senior Pastor
Bellevue Baptist Church
Memphis, Tennessee

Part I

SIGNIFICANCE OF LORDSHIP

O N E

The Book

If you miss being in the center of God's perfect will, you live your life without a cause, or live it for the wrong cause. You can go through life and believe that your life has never been really significant in any way.

This truth really hit home with me one night in Ho Chi Minh City (formerly Saigon), where I served as a missionary. Hunger overcame my desire to sleep. I decided that some *phu*—Vietnamese noodles—would be just the thing. I walked from my hotel to a nearby noodle shop. There I saw the book.

As the young man, who had cooked the hot chicken noodles, served them to me, he also handed me a book. It was filled with pictures that had once accompanied many newspaper articles.

Something about the book caused me to look and take notice of the room around me. One wall was decorated with a big plaque that the government had given the owner. It honored the owner's grandfather. It also contained an advertisement for an upper room in which one could spend the night for $15. It was said to be a very special room. One would be honored to sleep there.

"What is all of this?" I asked my young server.

Smiling, he said that the answer was contained in the book he had given to me.

While I ate my noodles, I read the book. It told the story of how the grandfather, the owner of the little shop, had served noodles there for more than 60 years. It also related how his life was characterized by more than noodles. This quiet, smiling little man was really a Viet Cong, committed to overthrowing the government of South Vietnam.

During their civil war, in which the United States of America was heavily involved, he bowed, smiled, and served our soldiers noodles in his little shop. At night, Viet Cong generals met in the room just above them. These insurgents were busy planning the famous 1968 Tet Offensive against Saigon.

While they lost that surprise attack, they really won, because this marked the turning point in the war. From that time, the communists knew that the Americans and South Vietnamese could be defeated. A failed attempt gave them the hope and inspiration they needed to continue their fight. The story of how a planning session in a little room above a noodle shop ended in the North Vietnamese victory was all in the book the man handed me.

Later that evening, I met the 91-year-old grandfather. As I walked back to my hotel, remembering the book and the plaque on the wall, I asked myself, "What is so special about that old man?"

Everything is in the eyes of the beholder. From my point of view, nothing was special about that individual. However, he played a key role in killing many young, American soldiers. In the eyes of the current government of Vietnam, he is a hero.

As I learned from the book, the quiet, little man in the noodle shop was not who or what he pretended to be. His country remembers him because he had a cause in which he believed. He used everything that he had to help his cause.

What about you? Ask yourself: When the books are opened someday regarding my life, what will they reveal? What is in my book? How can I discover meaning in and significance for my life?

TWO

Living to What End?

On a sunny December day, in the heart of a Brazilian summer, I did what I had done so many times during the 23 years Sherry and I had been married. I kissed her goodbye, climbed into my truck, and drove away to spend another weekend teaching and preaching. This time, however, things would never be the same again.

My destination was Viscosa, in the state of Minas Gerais. The First Baptist Church in the town was hosting a Pioneer Evangelism training conference. I would spend Friday night and all day Saturday teaching all the planned material. I had done this many times.

Throughout our married lives, I had made it a habit to call Sherry every night when I was away from home. On that Friday night, she concluded our conversation as she always did. She said, "I love you."

Those were the last words I would ever hear her speak.

By mid-morning on Saturday, something troubling happened to me. I was distracted by an inner voice that urgently told me to return home as soon as possible. I'm convinced that this was the Holy Spirit's prompting. I did not hesitate to obey. I told the pastor hosting me that I must return home immediately. I closed the conference at noon, got into my truck, and drove straight through to Belo Horizonte, our home.

When I pulled in front of our house, my youngest son, Jason, ran out the front door shouting, "Daddy, Daddy, we have got to get Mom to the hospital. Something just happened to her."

Rushing inside, I saw my beautiful, precious and wonderful wife lying dead on the bathroom floor.

Sherry had a very rare disease called scleroderma (see *www.scleroderma.org/fact.html*). This disease makes one's skin or internal organs turn as hard as stone. It is gradual and develops slowly. My wife's condition had been correctly diagnosed just one year before her death.

Those final months were ones of pain and torture. Often I would find her ravaged by diarrhea and vomiting at the same time. At other times, I had returned home to find her lying on our couch clutching her stomach in an attempt to ease the pain. She suffered so much in so many ways!

Through all of this agony, Sherry stayed at her post as a missionary. During the last month of her life, she hosted and served more than 200 meals and snacks to Brazilians, who were always in our home. She trained Brazilians to be interpreters for North American volunteers involved in missionary efforts. She conducted Bible studies and continued her teaching and discipleship ministries. She did not quit.

Knowing the pain she experienced, I wanted to leave the mission field and return to the United States. There, she could have been close to good medical care and near our two oldest children, who were students at Ouachita Baptist University in Arkansas. Finally, three months before she died, I said, "I believe that we should resign from the International Mission Board and return to the States."

"No," she replied. "The purpose of my life is to glorify Christ both in my life and in my death. God has called me to Brazil. I want to stay."

Sherry lived and died in the will of God. Her name is in The Book of Life.

I have no doubt that Sherry discovered what life is all about—what truly surrendering one's life to Christ in the fullest sense, to "be significant", to make a difference, means.

24

Because of this, her life had a lasting and eternal impact. It was given purpose and significance as she experienced the way and the Person who gives it to you. On her tombstone is written, "The purpose of my life is to glorify Christ both in my life and in my death."

What does having purpose—feeling significant—really mean?

THREE

The Promise

Bobby Welch, pastor and friend, once shared with me that in the depths of a dark tunnel is always light at the bottom. After Sherry died, I found that to be true. God's Word is filled with His promises. He is a true and faithful God plus a good friend in times of deep hurt, pain, and need.

We begin our new life in Christ by faith. Thus, we continue to walk by faith. We rely on His grace to sustain us through the journey. Christ calls. We decide whether to respond. Jesus called Peter and his brother, Andrew, when He said, "Come, follow me, and I will make you fishers of men" (Matt. 4:18-20). He called Matthew, the hated tax collector, and said, "follow me." Levi got up and followed him (Mark 2:14). He said to Zacchaeus, "come down immediately. I must stay at your house today." Nathaniel was a skeptic while he sat under a fig tree when Jesus called him (John 1:46-48).

Moses cried out, "Lord, please let someone else do it." Jeremiah cried out, "I do not know how to speak; I am only a child" (Jer. 1:6). In each of these cases, resistance occurred, but ultimately they followed Him.[1]

The call to follow Christ is a call to adventure. That journey sometimes leads one down a tough and dark path like it did me when Sherry died. On the other hand, it also leads one to experience a life of GRACE in the midst of trials and tribulations.

Grace is "God's free and undeserved mercy towards us." We often think of grace in regard to what we receive at the moment of salvation. Yet, it goes far beyond that. Grace is the means by which we survive through the hardships of life as we walk the adventure under the lordship of Christ.

After Sherry died, I thought I also would die. Yet, God's grace sustained me in many different ways. One of the main ways was that he pointed me to a beautiful woman named Barbara Hawthorne. Barbara was a missionary living in the same city of Belo Horizonte working with the churches in the area of human needs. She was a deeply spiritual believer in Christ. She was a strong witness for the Lord and a church planter. Barbara and Sherry had been dear friends. In fact, the day Sherry died, Sherry called Barbara and asked her to take care of her because she was feeling so bad. Barbara cooked a pizza for Sherry, read her a book, and watched a TV movie with her that day.

Before Sherry's death, Barbara and I knew each other only as colleagues in ministry. But after Sherry died, God began to speak to my heart that Barbara was in God's ultimate plan for my life. She would be a part of this adventurous journey to which he had called me. God knew my needs. He knew that I would someday need a life partner again.

I cannot point out the exact day or time that it occurred, but as I walked through this part of my journey, I began to sense the call of God on my life toward Barbara. One day I went to her and surprised her by saying, "Not now, but some-day you and I will get married". I am sure that almost knocked her off of her feet.

During that first year we became friends. I began to really seek God's will in this matter. Outside of following Christ, no more important decision exists in life than that of choosing a life partner. I was already 49 years old. I had three children. Two were in college. One was at home with me; I was Homeschooling him during his senior year in high school. Thus, I knew I could not make a mistake in this decision.

What did I do? I did what had now become a natural part of my life. I read the Word of God and waited on the Lord to give me a personal word from the Word. One day as I read Scripture, I read Jeremiah 29:11, "'For I know the plans I have for you,' declares the Lord, 'plans to prosper you and not to harm you, plans to give you hope and a future'" (NIV).

When I read that passage, God's Spirit just spoke to me in my spirit that Barbara was the one He had chosen for me. Here was the call. Now, I had to really decide. Should I really enter this marriage relationship with Barbara? I honestly began to really question myself, for this would be a major life step. Yet, I knew beyond a shadow of a doubt that God had spoken. I decided to go. I decided to follow Jesus.

A year after Sherry died, I gave Barbara an engagement ring at midnight on December 31, her birthday, as the New Year began. We were married eight months later—almost two years after Sherry had passed away.

Our marriage began a new adventure for both of us. We both took a large step of faith. That step was the beginning of a new call for both of us. That step of faith later was to take us both around the entire world as a husband-and-wife team proclaiming the gospel of Jesus Christ as Lord and Savior.

The call of Christ on one's life is a call to adventure. In this journey bad things do happen to good people. Yet, the grace of God is always there to sustain us. I learned that by saying "yes" to the call of living under the lordship of Christ, He has given me the greatest adventure in life.

[1]John R. Stott, *The Message of Ephesians: The Bible Speaks Today* (Leicester, England, and Downers Grove, IL: Inter-Varsity Press, 1979), 83.

FOUR

The Chess Game

You were never meant to live blundering through life in a random, hit-or-miss manner, hoping that something will eventually work out. God has a specific game plan—a strategy—for your life. As a student at Louisiana College in Pineville, Louisiana, I discovered just how important a good strategy can be. It gives meaning to every move that you make throughout every day.

Much to my dislike, in order to graduate from college, I was required to take one course in mathematics. Math is not my forte. As a high-school student, I kept at a minimum my encounters with the subject of math. In college, higher mathematics courses were seen as troubled waters. Because of this, when forced to do so, I chose the most basic course and prayed for a miracle.

My name, Akins, assured that my math professor's preference for alphabetical seating would put me front and center, on the front row of his classroom.

The one saving factor was that Gloria, the prettiest girl in the school, had a last name that began with "B." She was right up there with me, in seat number three. Only one student separated us; more about that later.

I did not take long to discover that my mathematics professor was an avid chess player. When he learned that the game is also one of my passions (as it is even to this day), he challenged me to a game. In fact, he did more than that. He said, "Akins, if you beat me two out of three games, I will raise your grade a full letter. If I beat you two out of three, I will lower it a full letter."

So, the great challenge between the student and the professor was on!

This was no private match, played quietly without witnesses. The venue was the freshman boy's dormitory. It was as rowdy and as public a place as you can imagine. When the first game began, bright-eyed college boys pressed in all around us.

That game was tough. At the end, I was surprised. I won!

Now, the pressure was really on. The second game was even more difficult. I sweated and squirmed my way through to defeat.

By this time, I was getting cold feet. I wasn't sure that I wanted to continue. The score was one to one. If I was going to quit, this was the time to do it.

Reason told me that with math skills lower than average, I could wind up making a "C" in my classwork and then have that lowered to a "D." Contemplating this spurred me to declare that I was ready to stop the tournament and call it a draw.

To my surprise, our audience of college boys began shouting, "No! Go for it! Go for it! Go for it! Don't quit! Take him on!"

Spurred on by my fans and against my better judgment, I went for it and took him on.

That third game was the toughest of all. My complete concentration and all of my limited skills were called into play. At the end, both the professor and the guys who had dared me to go on were in shock. I had won.

Living with Purpose

Chess is a game of purpose, strategy, and tactical maneuvering. The purpose is to capture the king.

Having an effective strategy means that you can see the big picture. Strategic rules teach you how to move your pieces. Knowing the power and limitations of each piece enables you to know what parts of the board are most important and how to plan your campaign. This compares to controlling the air or the hill during warfare. When you can see from the high ground, you know how to direct your attacks.

Tactical maneuvering is the small picture. When you have learned when and how to make the right maneuvers, you will know how to win the game on the ground. This is the hand-to-hand combat of chess. By mastering the principles of tactical maneuvering, you learn how and when to capture more of your opponent's pieces and pawns, in keeping with the big picture.

Which part of the game is most important? Chess is 90 percent tactical maneuvering. A great strategy is worthless if, in the heat of battle, you do not pick off your opponent's pieces when and where it will do your game the most good. The best plan is ruined if your opponent cripples you by capturing your queen.

Chess teaches many essential life principles For example, the game has an objective—a purpose. You have only one purpose: to capture the king.

Lives that win have a primary objective—a purpose. Yet, many people roam aimlessly through their lives with no clear sense of purpose. They play at life as a beginning chess player plays the game. Because they can't see the big picture, tactical maneuvering is a foreign concept. Their moves are impulsive and haphazard. These moves certainly have consequences, but most often the player is the victim and not the controller of his circumstances.

To beat an experienced player, think outside the lines of single threats. Make hidden multiple attacks. By moving one piece, threaten and attack several pieces at the same time. One move may have several hidden threats behind it. These are often difficult for even experienced players to detect. Multiple attacks allow you to think outside the lines of single threats while still playing within the rules.

Purpose, strategy, and tactics are all involved in chess. Life is like that. We have meaning and purpose when we know Christ in our lives personally. Christ was sent to earth to give Life and to give it more abundantly (with meaning and purpose). When you know Him personally, He will direct your life. He will give you both the overall strategy and daily tactics for fulfilling your purpose.

Proverbs 3:5-6 says, "Trust in the Lord with all your heart, and do not lean on your own understanding. In all your ways acknowledge Him, And He will make your paths straight."

Trusting Him is our strategy. As we do this, He will lead us in life's tactics—directing our paths moment by moment.

God has a strategy, a game plan, a purpose for your life. Can you put into one sentence your life's primary purpose?

Look at what Jesus said about His major goal in life. You cannot improve on what He said where a purpose statement is concerned. Addressing the Father in John 17:4, He said, "I glorified Thee on the earth, having accomplished the work which Thou hast given Me to do."

I have adopted that as the stated purpose of my life.

What does bringing glory to the Father mean? It means to give Him honor, worth, and praise. It means that the Living Creator God of this universe will reign supreme in each of us. He will sit on the throne of our lives. Our lives will reflect His presence; they will honor Him.

Notice the second thing Jesus said about His purpose. He said, "Having accomplished the work which Thou Hast given Me to do."

Many people begin running their life's race with real purpose. Only a few end the race with that purpose having been realized.

Do you want to begin and end well? Jesus did. He did not stop halfway. He was not a quitter. His stated goal was "to complete . . . accomplish" the work of the Father.

God wants to express Himself through you. He wants you to live all of your life, from beginning to end, with dynamic purpose and significance. He has a plan for you. Once discovered, your life will have meaning, purpose, and significance.

You probably wonder what happened in my Louisiana College math class. I made a "B", but my professor did not raise my grade to an "A." When I asked about this, he said, "Wade, you sat in seat number one. The girl who was next to you, in seat number two, quit college. That left a seat between you and Gloria, who was in seat number three. You sat there for a whole semester with one empty seat between you and the prettiest girl in the whole college. You did not have enough sense to move over next to her. So, I decided that anyone who is that stupid does not deserve an 'A' in my class."

FIVE

Standing in the Gap

One of my favorite Old Testament passages is Ezekiel 22: 26-31: "'Her priests have done violence to My law and have profaned My holy things; they have made no distinction between the holy and the profane, and they have not taught the difference between the unclean and the clean; and they hide their eyes from My sabbaths, and I am profaned among them. Her princes within her are like wolves tearing the prey, by shedding blood and destroying lives in order to get dishonest gain. And her prophets have smeared whitewash for them, seeing false visions and divining lies for them, saying, 'Thus says the Lord God,' when the Lord has not spoken.

"The people of the land have practiced oppression and committed robbery, and they have wronged the poor and needy and have oppressed the sojourner without justice. And I searched for a man among them who should build up the wall and stand in the gap before Me for the land, that I should not destroy it; but I found no one. Thus I have poured out My indignation on them; I have consumed them with the fire of My wrath; their way I have brought upon their heads,' declares the Lord God."

Ezekiel recounted God's description of the moral depravity of his nation. Because leaders had failed to give righteous leadership, judgment was inevitable. God's indictment spared no one. It included five specific groups that encompassed every segment of society.[1]

First, the priests were held responsible for national, moral, and spiritual disaster. They were to be the keepers of the Law, the guardians of the purity and holiness of the temple. Instead of guarding the temple, they were guilty of making it blasphemous and unclean. Instead of keeping the Law, they violated it. God said, "Her priests have done violence to My law and have profaned My holy things."

Next, God accused the princes. While these nobles from the ruling class of Judah were responsible for insuring law and order, they were only interested in personal gain.

Lying preachers were the third group to be held accountable by God. He said, "Her prophets have smeared whitewash for them, seeing false visions and divining lies for them, saying, 'Thus says the Lord God,' when the Lord has not spoken."

Men who were charged with being the moral and spiritual conscience of the nation refused to preach against the sin that was destroying it.

Government officials can be included in the accusations brought against the princes. These men, who were appointed to positions of trust, joined the corrupt nobles in destroying instead of building. God said that they were "like wolves tearing the prey, by shedding blood and destroying lives in order to get dishonest gain."

Finally, God charges the common person in the street with sharing in the moral destruction of the country. He said, "The people of the land have practiced oppression and committed robbery, and they have wronged the poor and needy and have oppressed the sojourner without justice."

In this environment of lying, greed, immorality, and shame, God looked for someone to take the lead and stand up for Him. He said, "I searched for a man among them who would build up the wall and stand in the gap before Me for the land, so that I would not destroy it; but I found no one."

God was looking for one person willing to go against the tide of national depravity—a man who would stand in His strength and be His voice.

Jerusalem was about to fall. Her walls would crumble, but already her moral and spiritual walls had been breached. A righteous and faithful man was needed to stand in this gap.

When no such man was found, the city's doom was sealed. God was ready to pour out His wrath and consume the Judeans with His fury.[2]

One person, in the right place at the right time, could have saved Jerusalem.

Have you ever wondered, "Does God really have a special place and purpose for me?" "Can my life have a special meaning and make a difference?"

God created you for a specific reason. For your life to have meaning and impact, discover God's purpose for your existence. Somewhere is a broken wall where you are meant to stand in the gap. He wants you to be His person in that place, for that purpose.

It all begins by a willful decision on one's part to commit himself or herself to the absolute control of the lordship of Christ. Lordship, simply defined, means that one will totally surrender to Christ for him to rule and reign over one's life.

To stand in the gap, one must totally understand his or her purpose and fully surrender his or her life to God through Christ. This means unconditional commitment to Him—nothing held back.

Don't worry about the job description. You may be a pastor, missionary, engineer, lawyer, school teacher, businessperson, construction worker, cowboy, or homemaker. If you are living in complete surrender to your Lord, you are making what could be a world of difference. All other life values, decisions, and actions flow from this basic core value. This is the bottom line.

[1]Lamar Eugene Cooper Sr., *Ezekiel, The New American Commentary* (Nashville: Broadman and Holman, 1994), 222.

[2]Ibid., 223.

Part II

SURRENDER
TO LORDSHIP

S I X

The Trail

What could be more beautiful? We were in the midst of Brazil's vast Amazon rain forest.

What could be more frightening? We were lost. How could this have happened?

During the 15 years that I had served as a missionary in Brazil, I had pleaded with my sister, Katherine, and her husband, Richard, to visit us. Finally, they agreed to do so. I was delighted.

Wanting this to be the experience of their lives, I arranged for an excursion down the Amazon River. This trip would include accommodations in the jungle. We booked with a company that maintained a nice cabin on the river. We were careful to obtain the services of an experienced professional guide who was exceedingly knowledgeable about ecology and botany.

Everything was in place to assure that nothing could go wrong. The trip could not have had a better beginning. We traveled by boat many miles down river to the idyllic location of our cabin. After settling in, we all went out for an afternoon of exploring. All around us, we saw beautiful, exotic birds, dense jungle foliage, and towering trees. We were in an unspoiled environment that one cannot adequately describe. That night things improved further. Without venturing far from the safety of our camp, we not only saw but caught several small alligators.

Everyone was excited the next morning when our guide announced that we were going for an extensive walk into the rain forest. We boated even farther down river and then were introduced to two local men who had agreed to take us deep into the jungle on a very non-tourist trail. Off we went, full of anticipation and confidence.

On the trail, we repeatedly met men emerging from the forest carrying large and heavy loads of manioc (a root which Brazilians cook or from which they make a flour to use in many recipes). Wanting to take us away from these signs of encroaching civilization, our guide suggested that we leave the trail. He pointed out that this would give him opportunities to explain more details about the trees, ecology, and life in the jungle. This sounded really exciting. We happily followed as our two local guides began using their long machetes to chop their way and create our own trail.

Our guide was in his element and glowed with enthusiasm as he expounded from his knowledge of the rain forest.

After an hour of following the hacking machetes, we were told that we must return to the main trail, find our boat, and return to our cabin in time for a nice, Amazon fishing trip. With even more adventure on the horizon, we followed the local guides as they turned and chopped in a new direction.

They chopped and chopped. We walked and walked. Slowly, after over an hour of chopping and walking, I began to understand our situation. Not wanting to alarm them, I said nothing to my sister and brother-in-law. Instead, I quietly told my wife, Barbara, "We are lost."

Speaking plainly, I asked our guide, "Are we lost?"

He said, "Yes, we are."

When you are lost deep in the world's largest primitive rain forest, what do you do? In three hours dark would fall. Then real trouble would begin. At night, exotic insects such as the dark corners of your house have never seen become aggressive. This is also when deadly snakes and poisonous spiders reign in this jungle. They are not just an annoyance.

They can make survival not only difficult but doubtful.

You've heard the warning: When in doubt, follow the "leaders." So, they chopped. We followed. The sound was almost melodic: chop, walk, chop, walk.

Finally, we arrived at a small footpath. I insisted that we stay on that trail and walk wherever it would lead. We turned left and began a long walk. We hoped it would take us out of and not deeper into this wilderness.

After some time on the footpath, our local guides said, "We recognize where we are now. We can leave this trail and take a short cut back through the jungle."

Common sense and every impulse within me totally opposed this. Leave the trail? Not on my life. But our "highly competent" professional guide said, "Wade, we cannot let your fear deter us."

So, they chopped and we all walked . . . in a big circle. They were confused and lost. We were the blind following the blind.

Mercifully, we crossed our footpath again. This time, I absolutely insisted that we turn left and stay on this trail until we got out of this jungle.

When we arrived at a clearing, I told my sister, "This is a good sign. It means farmers are near. We are close to civilization."

So much for the missionary being a great wilderness scout; we had simply arrived at a natural clearing in the forest that had nothing to do with human hands. Seated in the middle of this 100-yard circle, we were not only still lost but, once again, we had lost our trail.

Feeling the full gravity of our situation, I approached one of the local guides and told him, "You have got to find that trail."

He did.

When we arrived at a body of water, we grasped it as a good sign. At least we would not die of dehydration!

While we watched in amazement, one of our local guides

walked into the water, waded across, and kept going. As we watched him disappear into the rain forest, we opted for taking a longer but drier way around. At last we found a more convenient crossing.

Meanwhile, our departed guide stood in the forest shouting, "Help! Help! Help! Help!" as loudly as possible. Miraculously, workers cutting sugar cane a mile or so away managed to barely hear his cries and walked to him. Soon, rowing a leaky log canoe, they arrived to rescue us.

With great apprehension, one by one we maneuvered into the crude, dugout boat, crossed over to solid land, and tried to look confident as we continued on another trail.

This time our hope was rewarded. We arrived at a small river community where men were loading a sugar-cane boat that was headed for Manaus, the only urban sanctuary in Brazil's vast rain forest region.

We had left our camp that morning in search of adventure. Now, we had more than we could have imagined. Under a full moon, we perched on top of the sugar cane and cruised for four hours down one of the world's most awesome waterways. What a ride! What a night!

What was being lost in the rain forest really like?

Above all else, it gave me a new comprehension of lostness. Now, I understand the situation of a person who is spiritually lost—seemingly without hope. The really frightening thing is that you do not know your future. You are at the mercy of a hostile environment and without a clear sense of direction.

Our hope returned when we found the trail. The trail was the answer.

Being lost spiritually in the jungle of sin is to be without hope until one finds the Trail—Jesus Christ. Jesus said, "I am the way, the truth, and the life. No one comes to the Father except through Me" (John 14:6, NKJV).

He did not say He is a way. He said that He is The Way.

For us, one way existed out of the Amazon wilderness—

only one. When our guides decided to leave that way—to get off the trail and chop their own way out—we got lost again. The key to our survival was to have faith in the trail.

Jesus, who is both our Lord and Savior, is our Way out of being lost.

Why is Jesus the only Way? Jesus is the only Way, because of what He did on the cross for our sins.

SEVEN

"Kill Me"

Almost 2,000 people had gathered in the city plaza of Neponecema, Minas Gerais, Brazil, to see the Jesus film produced by Campus Crusade for Christ. That evening, I would show the final part of the movie, depicting the crucifixion of Christ. I would bring a brief message about the cross and invite people to give their lives to Jesus as their Lord and Savior.

The film captured everyone's attention. No one moved. Every eye followed the scene showing the Roman soldiers driving nails into the hands and feet of Jesus. As the nails pierced His feet, many people in the crowd began to weep. The eyes of others were squeezed tightly shut, as though they could vicariously feel the pain that Jesus had endured. Throughout the crowd, emotions were high.

Suddenly, a man ran toward our truck, on which was mounted a metal screen and a special curtain for showing the film. Before anyone could move to stop him, he leaped up and grasped the screen with both of his hands. Shaking the screen back and forth, he shouted in Portuguese, *"Mate me! Mate me! Mate me!"*

These are the Portuguese words for, "Kill me! Kill me! Kill me!"

He did not want Jesus to die. He wanted to die in His place.

The man got it wrong. He wanted to die in Jesus' place but, 2,000 years ago, our Lord had already died in his place

44

and ours. By going to the cross, Jesus was saying, "Kill me! Kill me! Kill me!"

Sin requires the payment of a penalty. This payment is death. In order for our sins to be forgiven, someone had to die. We could not pay the penalty and have any hope.

God's good news is this: Christ died in our place. He paid the price for us.

His was no ordinary death. The gospel, the good news, is summed up in 1 Corinthians 15:3-4, " . . . that Christ died for our sins according to the Scriptures, and that He was buried, and that He was raised on the third day according to the Scriptures."

People shouted, "Kill Jesus!"

However, neither the angry mob, the religious leaders, nor the Roman soldiers were in control of what happened at the cross. God the Father allowed His Son, Jesus, to die and pay the penalty for your sins and mine. The purpose of Jesus' being sent to earth was to die for our redemption; it was the only way.

Jesus died voluntarily. He did for us what we could not do for ourselves. He died in our place.

He not only died for us, but He also conquered death and is wonderfully alive. This is why He alone can say, "I am the way, and the truth, and the life; no one comes to the Father but through Me" (John 14:6).

What happened on the cross must be understood and applied in your life, because it is the key element of the Christian life. Apart from this, one cannot become a Christian and live a victorious life. At the cross, you were redeemed; your salvation was secured.

God bought you with the blood of Jesus Christ. Now, as a believer, you belong to Him. You are His adopted child and a citizen of His Kingdom.

Three Biblical terms (reconcile, redeem, and justification) clearly explain what the death of Christ on the cross accomplished for you and me and why Jesus is the only Way.

Reconciliation:
Pig Eye

While Barbara and I were in Hanoi, Vietnam, we visited the Hanoi Hilton Hotel. This was actually the prison in which the North Vietnamese held our captured American soldiers during the Vietnam War.

When the Viet Cong shot down a North American pilot and captured him, he was treated as an enemy. He received no pardon, no forgiveness. Normally, the prisoner was tortured.

Captain Howard Rutledge shared his experiences of being tormented in the Hanoi Hilton. He recalled one particular North Vietnamese soldier whom the prisoners named Pig Eye.

Pig Eye forced Captain Rutledge to sit on the ground in a torturous position. His legs became so swollen that he was not able to extend them. The cruel interrogator then placed one of his heavy boots on his prisoner's knee and forced it downward. Afterward he chained the suffering American's legs together in stocks. A cane and heavy rope were used to lock the ankles in place. Next, he tied his victim's wrists behind his back. A guard would put his foot into the secured man's back and pull on the rope until the bound arms were almost separated from their sockets.

Captain Rutledge said he could feel the rope cutting his wrist to the bones. The pain was so great that he would ask God to let him slip into unconsciousness.[1]

This is how people treat their enemies. We can be thankful that God is different. When His enemies approach Him, they are reconciled by what Christ did on the cross. This is His good news for all people.

In Romans 5:10, Paul was inspired to write, "For if while we were enemies, we were reconciled to God through the death of His Son, much more, having been reconciled, we shall be saved by His life."

Commenting on this, William Barclay wrote, "The essence of Christianity is the restoration of a lost relationship."[2]

When the New Testament speaks of reconciliation, it addresses a broken relationship with someone you know personally. A barrier has been set up between you and that individual, to the point that you look on one another as enemies. To eliminate that barrier is to restore the relationship completely—to be reconciled.

"Reconcile" carries the idea of change.[3] On the cross of Christ, God changed our relationship with Him from hostility to peace.

A.T. Robertson, a noted Greek scholar, says, "Paul did not conceive that it was his or our work to reconcile God to us. God already took care of this himself."[4]

Only one way existed for the hostility which humanity has toward God to be removed. God Himself took the initiative. He sent Christ to die on the cross for our sins. Through His death, the barrier between God and man was torn down.

In 2 Corinthians 5:19, Paul wrote, "that God was in Christ reconciling the world to Himself, not counting their trespasses against them, and He has committed to us the word of reconciliation."

Christianity's primary message is this: Jesus of Nazareth died on a cross to destroy the barrier between God and humankind. Through His sacrificial death, the barrier of sin was removed. Now, humanity can approach God, be forgiven, and have relationship with God restored.

In 2 Corinthians 5:17 the Bible says, "Therefore if any man is in Christ, he is a new creature; the old things passed away; behold, new things have come."

Eduardo

Eduardo is a Brazilian friend. Before we met, he had lived a rough and perverse life. By his own testimony, he had done everything bad short of murder, including drug use and homosexuality. He was definitely an enemy of God. Then, one night, he cried out and asked Jesus for forgiveness. Christ entered his life. He was radically changed. The barrier between him and God was demolished. His guilt and shame had already been placed on his Savior when He died on the cross. Because of that, my friend could be reconciled to God. Today, he is a new person in Christ—a minister of the gospel of Christ. Today he shares the message of reconciliation. This is our message of good news for a world that seems to be without hope.

As a believer, you can only have the cleansing of sin and a sense of reconciliation with God on the basis of the finished work of Christ on the cross.

Redemption:
The Trail of Tears

While I preached in the West African nation of Benin, I discovered this amazing story. In the fifteenth century existed a people group called the Xwedah. Today they are known as the *Quidah*—a French word which means "help." They can be found in Benin.

A Xwedah king, Kpasse, built a palace near the beach so he could better monitor his field workers. This is the site of the present city of Quidah. When Europeans first arrived in West Africa, King Kpasse's farm became their main trade center. The place was marked for infamy.

A Spanish priest, Bartholome Las Cassas, had observed the strength of the African people. He was desperate to save the natives of the Americas from forced labor by their European conquerors. He successfully proposed to replace them with African workers. Pope Nicolas V signed the first slave trade agreement in 1454. This launched centuries of living hell for Africans.

From that point, millions of Africans were killed or deported to work as slaves in the newly conquered Americas.

They were used to fuel the agricultural economies of Brazil, the United States, and the Caribbean.

Local kings soon saw how they could benefit from this horrible business of selling men and women. To expand their kingdoms, they needed the guns, cannons, and gunpowder that the Europeans brought them. To secure these, they sold the captives from their local wars to the white traders.

In 1727, King Agadja conquered Quidah. He made it the center of his trade in human cargo with the Europeans. At first, he was content to sell defeated enemies, but his consumers were greedy. They demanded more and more slaves. Soon, commando units were raiding villages, capturing men, women, boys, and girls. Anyone who resisted was killed.

In chains, these captives were marched to Quidah, in what is now South Benin. They were made to walk only at night. This was not only to escape the tropical heat but to keep anyone from finding his or her way way back to that person's village. Crying in pain and despair, they were hidden in the bush during the daylight. From the moment of their capture, they received no mercy. Many of these people died before they ever reached Quidah.

Once there, slave traders from Portugal, France, England, Holland, and Denmark bid for them under a huge tree in the center of the city. From this market the slaves were led down a path to the ocean, where the ships were waiting to haul them to foreign lands. They were allowed one last stop at what was called "The Tree of Return." They were allowed to walk around the tree three times, in the hope that their spirits would one day return to Africa. This was their last ritual before they passed through the "Door of No Return."[5]

Suppose a slave was taken to the Americas and bought by a good and merciful man. The master then would tell the slave, "I have purchased you with my money, but I am going to give to you a gift of freedom."

A lost sinner is in exactly the position of the slaves that I have just described. Without Christ, a person is without hope.

When he turns his back on God and becomes the slave of sin, he passes through the "Door of No Return." But, miracle of miracles, Jesus paid the highest price possible—the price of His own blood—to purchase the slave! Because of this, hope exists where no hope existed. The sinner can be set free.

This is redemption—buying a hopeless slave, with a price, and setting that slave free.

Redeem is another word that describes what happened when Jesus died on the cross. As it is used in the Bible, it means "to free by ransom."

An Old Testament law said if a man owned a bull that had a habit of goring people, the animal must be securely confined. If the owner did not keep his bull penned up and it killed someone, both the bull and the owner were to be stoned to death. However, the law allowed for a payment to be made to redeem the man's life. He was required to pay whatever was demanded of him.[6]

Decades later, Job declared, "I know that my Redeemer lives" (Job 19:25).

In the New Testament the word *redeem* is used with the reference to slave markets. The thought was that a payment had to be made in order for a slave to be freed.

Jesus said, "For even the Son of Man did not come to be served, but to serve, and to give His life a ransom for many" (Mark 10:45).

Paul used this word when he wrote, "In Him we have redemption through His blood, the forgiveness of our trespasses, according to the riches of His grace" (Eph. 1:7).

He was saying that we are set free from slavery to sin by the sacrificial death of Christ on the cross. With His own blood Jesus paid our ransom.

In 1 Peter 1:18-19, the Bible says, "knowing that you were not redeemed with perishable things like silver or gold from your futile way of life inherited from your forefathers, but with precious blood, as of a lamb unblemished and spotless, the blood of Christ."

When you surrender your life to Christ, from time to time you will still sin, but when Jesus died on the cross, He paid for all of your sins—once and for eternity. Because of this, you can be cleansed and made holy before God.

Fanny Crosby wrote this great hymn about redemption:
"Redeemed, how I love to proclaim it!
Redeemed by the blood of the Lamb;
Redeemed by his infinite mercy,
His child, and forever I am."[7]

Justification:
A Murderer's Prayer

Our town marshal had asked me to accompany him as he answered an emergency call. We drove into the darkness of the Louisiana countryside and stopped where four bodies blocked the lonely gravel road. Each of these people had been shot in the head. For many days, their blood would mark the spots where they had died.

Quickly, a posse formed to assist the police. Heavily armed and using dogs to follow the murderer's scent, these men searched throughout the night. Early the next morning, they found the suspect hiding in a barn. They took him to the Clinton Parish jail to wait for his arraignment and trail.

Since my sophomore year in high school, I had preached every Sunday at the parish jail. The Sunday after the murders was no exception.

That morning, I told the prisoners that despite what crimes they had committed, God would forgive them if they would repent and trust Christ as their Lord and Savior. I invited those who wanted to give their lives to Christ to kneel on the floor in front of me. Slowly, from the back of the room, a man walked forward. He dropped to his knees in front of me and began to weep. Through his tears, he said, "I am sorry for what I did. Will God forgive me?"

Amazed, I realized that the broken man before me was the murderer of the people whose bodies I had seen on that country road.

"Yes," I assured him. "No sin exists that God cannot forgive."

That day, I watched as a murderer prayed and asked Christ to forgive him and to enter his heart.

Was it real? Only he and God know that. I do know this: If he meant what he prayed, God took his sin of murder and placed it on Christ. Christ bore on the cross the man's sin of murder.

When Jesus died on the cross, He was punished for the murders that the man committed. He was judged and condemned for killing those people. All of the prisoner's guilt was placed on Jesus, even though He was righteous and without sin.

Here is what happened: In His body, Christ suffered all the guilt and punishment which the murderer deserved.

Remember the introduction to this chapter and the lesson of Romans 5:1. When the guilty man cried out and received Jesus as his Lord and Savior, God placed in him His own righteousness.

When, on Judgment Day, that murderer goes before God the Father, He will not see the man's sin of murder, or any other sin. He will see the righteousness of Christ in that man. The Father will look into his heart and see His Son, Jesus Christ. For that reason only, He will say to him, "Welcome into my house." The Bible calls this transfer "justification".

Justified is the Bible's legal term for what it means to "be saved."

In The Amplified Bible, Romans 5:1 reads, "Therefore, since we are justified—acquitted, declared righteous, and given a right standing with God—through faith, let us [grasp the fact that we] have [the peace of reconciliation] to hold and to enjoy, peace with God through our Lord Jesus Christ, the Messiah, the Anointed One."

Someone may protest that words such as justification are theological jargon which they cannot understand. An old-fashioned definition puts the cookies on the bottom shelf, where everyone can reach them. Justification means that God will treat me "just as if I'd" never sinned and just as if I had perfectly obeyed.

When you are justified, the guilt and penalty of your sin are removed. Christ's own righteousness is imparted to you. In other words, when God the Father looks into your heart, instead of the ugliness of your sin, He sees the righteousness of His Son.

Justified is a legal term that describes what happens when you receive Christ as your personal Lord and Savior (John 1:12). When you are justified, your judicial standing is changed before God.

An accused man stands in court and waits for the jury to pronounce its verdict. When the foreman stands and reads "not guilty," the man is instantly declared innocent of all charges against him. He will walk out of the courtroom a free person. He is justified.

Being justified before God means more than being declared "not guilty." It means that you are declared to be righteous. God places the perfect righteousness of Jesus Christ into your heart.

Galatians 3:6 (The Amplified Bible) reads, "Abraham believed and adhered to and trusted in and relied on God, and it was reckoned and placed to his account and accredited as righteousness—as conformity to the divine will in purpose, thought, and action."

This word *credited* is *imputed* in the Greek New Testament (*logizomai*). It means to count—to reckon, calculate, and compute—to set to one's account. Abraham believed God. His act of faith was placed on deposit for him and valued as righteousness. This does not mean he deserved this reward. That would be salvation by works. He simply cast all of his dependence on God and accepted God's way of salvation.[8]

In Romans 4:6 and 8, the Bible says, "Just as David also speaks of the blessing on the man to whom God credits righteousness apart from works . . . Blessed is the man whose sin the Lord will not take into account."

Verses 22-25 say, "Therefore it was also reckoned to him as righteousness. Now not for his sake only was it written, that it was credited to him, but for our sake also, to whom it will be credited, as those who believe in Him who raised Jesus our Lord from the dead, He who was delivered over because of our transgressions, and was raised because of our justification."

The words *it was credited to him* were not written for Abraham alone. It was also written for all of us who believe on God the Father, who raised Jesus from the dead. Because of our trust in Christ, our accounts will be credited with His righteousness.

You may look at yourself and ask, "How can that be? I know myself. By nature and by choice, I am a sinner. I don't deserve to be justified."

To understand the miracle of justification, by faith, accept these truths. Jesus Christ lived a sinless life. He was perfect. Yet, He died a criminal's death on a cross, as if He were a sinner. Why? Because, at the moment of His death, God the Father placed on Jesus all of our sin. He took upon Himself the full weight of your guilt and mine. He went to the cross without sin, so that He could redeem you from the penalty and power of sin. He died for you.

In Romans 5:19, the Apostle Paul wrote about this truth. "For as through the one man's disobedience the many were made sinners, even so through the obedience of the One the many will be made righteous."

In 1 Corinthians 1:30, we read: "But by His doing you are in Christ Jesus, who became to us wisdom from God, and righteousness and sanctification, and redemption."

Don't misunderstand what this means. Justification does not make you righteous, but you are declared righteous because of the righteousness of Christ that is in you as a free gift from God.

Romans 3:24 says that we are "being justified as a gift by His grace through the redemption which is in Christ Jesus."

Be sure that you fully digest what is being said here. Justification is a gift from God. It is granted by grace, the unmerited favor of God. By definition any gift is free. It cannot be earned. A gift of grace is one that is offered not only to someone who has not earned it; he does not deserve it. When you receive Christ into your life, two things happen. First, your sins leave you and are placed on Jesus. Secondly, the righteousness of Christ enters your heart. An exchange takes place. Christ exchanges His righteousness for your sins. What an incredible exchange this is: our sins for His righteousness!

In 1 John 5:12-13, the Bible says, "He who has the Son has the life; he who does not have the Son of God does not have the life. These things I have written to you who believe in the name of the Son of God, so that you may know that you have eternal life."

Ask yourself, "Do I know that I have the Son, am I justified—saved by grace through faith in Christ (Eph. 2:8-9)?"

Even a murderer can know this.

How can you know that you have the Son—that you are justified? Read on.

[1]Howard and Phyllis Rutledge, *In the Presence of Mine Enemies* (Old Tappan, NJ: Fleming H. Revell, 1973), 25.

[2]William Barclay, *New Testament Words* (Philadelphia: Westminster Press, 1974), 168.

[3]Kenneth S. Wuest, *Wuest's Studies from the New Testament Greek* (Grand Rapids: Wm. B. Eerdmans, 1953), 82.

[4]Archibald Thomas Robertson, *Word Pictures in the New Testament, Vol. IV* (Grand Rapids: Baker Book House, 1931), 357.

[5]Martine de Souza, *Regard sur Ouidah: A Bit of History* (Ouidah, Benin, Africa), 35-39.

[6]Exodus 21:29-30.

[7]Words to the hymn "Redeemed, How I Love to Proclaim It" by Fanny Crosby, Public Domain.

[8]Kenneth S. Wuest, *Romans in the Greek New Testament: Wuest's Word Studies for the English Reader* (Grand Rapids: Eerdmans, 1955), 67.

EIGHT

"I Love You. I Love You. I Love You."

When the gospel (the good news about Jesus) is preached, the Holy Spirit calls for sinners to become one with God through Christ.

God's part was sending His only begotten Son to die a violent, bloody, sacrificial death as a substitute for our sins. Our part is to receive Christ and His pardon. This requires two things: repentance and faith.

Often, when I think about this response to the gospel message, I remember Gladys Johnson.

The day in the Washington, D.C., area was cold and rainy. My youth band was scheduled for a concert in the parking lot of the Rose Hill Shopping Center in Springfield, Virginia.

Our group played Christian contemporary, semi-folk, and rock music. On the weekends we conducted evangelistic, concert-style programs throughout the Washington area. Our sole purpose was to reach people who did not attend church. We reached out to hippies and other young people who drank and took drugs as they hung around the malls.

Our format was always the same. The group sang and played. Its cutting-edge music about Christ always attracted a crowd. At some point in the concert, I stepped up to the microphone and brought an evangelistic message. It wasn't the kind of sermon you would expect to hear in church. I never used a Bible. I always began by telling a shocking, true story in order to gain the attention of the crowd. I used stories to explain the gospel. I preached for about 10 minutes. I concluded by inviting listeners to walk to where I was standing, kneel on the pavement, and give their lives to Christ. In these open-air meetings we saw many young people commit their lives to Him.

This cold day was extremely unusual. One of our lead singers called to say that she was sick. Another singer called to tell me that she had the flu. Our drummer, one of our guitar players, and another singer were all unavailable. That left me with Jeff Thornley, a guitar player and singer, and David Weaver, who helped set up and manage the electrical equipment.

We sat in my apartment and asked ourselves, "What should we do?"

Clearly, the Holy Spirit said to me, "Go anyway."

When I told the other guys this, they both agreed to give it a try.

We went to the shopping center and set up the equipment in the light rain and cold. Jeff sang a song, but no one seemed attracted to form a crowd around us. I am not a singer, but I tried singing one song with him. In protest, someone blew a car horn at us. Things were really bad.

After Jeff had tried one more song, he turned to me and said, "You need to preach."

When I stepped up to the microphone, no one was in front of me. I faced a wet and empty parking lot. I asked myself, "What am I doing?"

In my heart, I knew that God was telling me to preach, so I preached to the air. I felt stupid. I had never preached to empty air before. Still, I preached diligently and with conviction.

As usual, I concluded with an altar call. I merely said, "If anyone is listening, and you want to give your life to Christ, step up here now and pray with me."

Suddenly, on the other side of the parking lot, a car door opened. A woman stepped out. She was walking slowly, but she walked straight toward me. She knelt on the wet pavement at my feet. I knelt with her as she prayed and gave her heart to Christ.

When we had finished praying and were standing, she grabbed me around the neck and began to shout, "I love you! I love you! I love you!"

While she did this, I smelled alcohol on her breath and thought to myself, "Ma'am, you are drunk."

In a moment such as that, the devil can get all over what is happening. I was tempted to think that her commitment to Christ was not real and that, when she was sober, all of this would be empty and forgotten. These are the times when we need to hear the Holy Spirit saying, "Not so fast."

Later, Gladys Johnson wrote to tell me that when she heard me preaching to the empty parking lot, she was on her way home to commit suicide. She thought that she had tried everything life offered in an effort to find peace. Nothing had worked. She had gotten to the point of no hope. Then, she saw us out there on the parking lot and decided to listen. She said that when I stood to preach she was thinking, "If what he is saying does not give me hope, I will kill myself today."

Gladys joined the Calvary Road Baptist Church in her Virginia community and became a leader in the children's ministry. God used her to lead her husband, Bill, and nine members of her family to Christ.

Twenty-five years later, while on Stateside missionary assignment from Brazil, I preached one evening in a small, rural church in Grove, Virginia. I was there at the invitation of Pastor Ronnie Roach. Barbara and I arrived a little late and found the church filled with people. Suddenly, I heard a voice I had not heard in a quarter of a century. A woman walked toward me shouting, "I love you. I love you. I love you."

It was Gladys. What she had discovered on that cold, wet, mall parking lot was still real and life-transforming. She had heard that we were to be in Grove. She had driven across the state of Virginia to see me.

Often when I hesitate to seize an unlikely evangelistic opportunity, I remember her beautiful words: "I love you. I love you. I love you."

Those words sprang from the heart of someone who thought she had tried everything until, through a man who thought he was preaching to no one, she heard Jesus say, "Come, follow me."

She did. Her hopelessness turned to hope. She had been justified by the pure and loving grace of God.

Repentance and Faith

When Gladys heard the good news about Jesus, she repented. By faith, she received Him as her Lord and Savior.

Repentance means *to change your mind*. When you repent, you change your mind about who God is, about sin, and about Jesus Christ. It also means *to turn*. You turn from a self-controlled life to Jesus Christ, who is Lord.

Changing your own life through self-effort is impossible. Repentance is not your own determination to modify your behavior or to change the way you are living and do better. It is your turning to Christ and allowing Him to take complete control of your life. He does all of the changing.

Repentance and faith cannot be separated. When the Holy Spirit convicts and draws you, He enables you to repent, to turn from sin, and to commit yourself, by faith, to Christ.

Faith is more than an intellectual, head knowledge and belief that God exists and that Jesus died for your sins. Biblical faith requires a total commitment of your life to Christ. Surrender to Him as your Lord and Master.

In Romans 10:9, Paul stressed that being a Christian means that you acknowledge that Jesus is Lord. In The Amplified Bible that verse reads, "Because if you acknowledge and confess with your lips that Jesus is Lord and in your heart believe (adhere to, trust in, and rely on the truth) that God raised Him from the dead, you will be saved."

This verse talks about "heart belief" ("in your heart believe"). This means that you trust Christ to do for you what you cannot do for yourself—forgive your sins and transform your life.

When you are convinced that Jesus is Lord and you confess this openly, you are drawn to turn in repentance from your self-controlled life and to surrender completely to Jesus as Lord. You allow Him to take absolute control of your life.

Most Bible scholars recognize three aspects of faith: knowledge (*notitia*), assent (*assensus*), and trust (*fiducia*). Theologian Augustus H. Strong sees knowledge as the intellectual element of faith. Assent is the emotional element. Trust is the volitional element.[1]

True faith involves all three elements. First, your mind embraces the knowledge of who Christ is—that He died on a cross as a sacrifice for your sins and that He rose from the dead. Next, you assent (agree) to this truth in your heart. You feel in your innermost being that this is true. Finally, you make a decision, by your own will, to commit yourself to Christ. You invite Him to take control of your life.

You cannot divide Jesus into two entities—Savior or Lord. He is Savior and Lord. You cannot receive half of Jesus. Accept Him for all that He is.

Jesus is also God, King, Judge, Advocate (Supporter), and Counselor. He is the Alpha and the Omega (the Beginning and the End). Jesus is all of this and more. When you receive Christ, accept and trust Him for all that He is.

When you are committed to Jesus as your Lord and Savior, you are saved. You are justified. You are a child of God. Your sins are forgiven. Christ's righteousness has been planted in your heart.

It all begins with one word—*surrender*. God requires unconditional surrender.

Noted author John MacArthur says, "Surrender to Jesus' lordship is not an addendum to the biblical terms of salvation: the summons to submission is at the heart of the gospel invitation throughout Scripture."[2]

He concludes that surrender is not an addition to faith but is "the essence of faith."[3]

Trust is the essential factor in surrender. Pastor and author Rick Warren says, "You will not surrender to God unless you trust Him."[4]

Whatever you are surrendered to defines your life. All of us are the sum of our commitments. In order to have purpose and meaning, be committed to the right thing. In this case, the right thing is really not a thing but a person—Jesus Christ.

God is looking for people whom He can use. God is looking in all of our hearts to see on whom He can depend to make differences in the world for His glory. If you want God to use you, one requirement exists. 2 Chronicles 16:9 says, "For the eyes of the Lord move to and fro throughout the earth that He may strongly support those whose heart is completely His." Take notice that God looks for that person "whose heart is completely His." In other words, He looks for a person who is totally surrendered to Him.

God has a primary purpose for your life. He will not force Himself on you. He gives you a choice. This is where surrender (commitment) comes in. Before anything else can happen, you must know God, turn in repentance, receive Christ by faith, and be totally committed to Him as your Lord. In other words, you need to become a 24/7 Christian.

This is the most important issue in your life.

Every commitment has a benefit and a cost. What's the cost of following Christ? You give up the control of your life and put Jesus Christ in charge.

Have you settled this matter of Christ's lordship and your relationship to Him? If not, right now, do what Gladys Johnson did. She stepped forward, just as she was, and gave her life completely to Christ.

Before you close this book, pray simply and humbly to Jesus. From your heart, say, "Lord Jesus Christ, I open my heart to you. I surrender myself to you for the rest of my life."

Charlotte Elliott's great hymn of invitation expresses our only way to Christ:

"Just as I am, without one plea,
But that Thy blood was shed for me,
And that Thou bidst me come to Thee-
O Lamb of God, I come, I come!"

You trust Him with all your doubts and fears—just as you are.

The path toward lordship ends at the cross when you lay down all of your sin at the feet of Jesus. If you prayed this prayer, He has taken away the barrier between you and the Father. Now, you can be clean and holy.

Your life will now have new meaning. You will be walking in a new direction. You will see the world through new eyes. Your value system will be radically changed.

2 Corinthians 5:17 says, "Therefore if any man is in Christ, he is a new creature; the old things passed away; behold, new things have come."

You have now begun a new exciting journey as God will mold your life to become what you were created to be. Philippians 1:6 (NIV) says, "being confident of this, that he who began a good work in you will carry it on to completion until the day of Christ Jesus."

[1]Augustus H. Strong, *Systematic Theology* (Philadelphia: Judson, 1907), 837-838.

[2] John MacArthur, *The Gospel According to the Apostles* (Nashville: Word Publishing, 1993), 23.

[3]Ibid., 30.

[4]Rick Warren, *The Purpose-Driven Life* (Grand Rapids: Zondervan, 2002), 78.

Part III

STRUGGLING WITH LORDSHIP

NINE

The Lion Within

By struggling with the issues of life, and against the dominance of self, you grow spiritually. Through your dependence on Christ, you learn to yield to His lordship. Without these struggles, you will not grow as His disciple.

However, while this spiritual striving is as vital to the development of spiritual strength as physical exercise is to the development of physical strength, remember that the battle cannot be won simply through your earnest effort.

For most earnest Christians, the norm is to "do your best for God." This isn't good enough. Living a victorious Christian life in your own strength is impossible.

If you want to experience success and power as a Christian, understand that a battle is being waged in your heart.

You may have explained your conversion experience to someone by saying, "Jesus entered my heart."

This is true, but how can it be? Jesus died for our sins, was buried and, on the third day, He was raised from the dead. He returned to heaven and is now at the right hand of the Father, making intercession for us. So, how can He be in heaven and in our hearts at the same time?

He is in our hearts by means of the Holy Spirit. The Holy Spirit entered your heart the moment you gave your life to Christ.

Paul wrote, "If anyone does not have the Spirit of Christ, he does not belong to Him" (Rom. 8:9).

According to the Bible, we all have sin residing in us. The Bible uses the word *sin* in several different ways. It can mean specific acts of sin, such as lust, lying, or stealing. It can also be used in reference to our sinful nature.

My wife, Barbara, and I spend much of our time ministering in Africa. One of our great pleasures is to go to the game reserves and see the animals in the wild. We always go hoping that we will see lions. Why? Because lions are the kings of the beasts. Their majesty and power are overwhelming.

Suppose you took a baby lion and tried to make it into a domestic pet. You could feed it milk, pet it, and love it. Perhaps it would seem to love you in return. The great cat would grow into adulthood. Then, one day, without any warning, your "pet" suddenly could turn and kill you. Why? The animal you tried to domesticate had a wild nature.

It is the same with us. We grow up as seemingly innocent babies but, in reality, we are not innocent. We have within us a sinful and evil nature. When we grow up, our nature is to break the laws of God.

No one has to teach us how to sin. We do it naturally.

Once we give our lives to Christ, the Holy Spirit lives within us, but we have now two natures. We have a new life and a new nature, but we still have our old nature, which the Bible calls "the flesh."

When you received Christ as your Savior, the penalty for your sin was paid. Your self-nature was dethroned as the king of your heart. You entered into a vital union with Jesus for eternity. Christ died for you, but you also died with Him. Your old self died. You were spiritually raised to a new life in Him. God planted His own divine nature in you.

In Romans 6:4, Paul was inspired to explain it in this way: "Therefore we have been buried with Him through baptism into death, in order that as Christ was raised from the dead through the glory of the Father, so we too might walk in newness of life."

Two things happened when you became a Christian. You died to your evil nature. You were raised to a new life.

Any believer who tries to live without depending on this new divine nature will be defeated.

Two Big Questions

You may be asking the big question: "Sin is still so real and powerful within me! How can I live controlled by my new spiritual nature?"

You must learn to be Spirit-controlled instead of self-controlled.

Paul confessed, "For I know that nothing good dwells in me, that is, in my flesh; for the wishing is present in me, but the doing of the good is not. For the good that I wish, I do not do, but I practice the very evil that I do not wish" (Rom. 7:18-19).

In your own strength, you try and try to do that which is right. The more diligently you try, the more you fail. Finally, you realize that this life is impossible in and of yourself. Eureka! Once you have made that discovery, you have taken the first step toward experiencing victory and power.

Until this happens, you will fail again and again. You will become more and more frustrated.

In Romans 7:15, Paul expressed his dilemma: "For that which I am doing, I do not understand; for I am not practicing what I would like to do, but I am doing the very thing I hate."

Paul was saying that he wanted to live a victorious life, but try as he might, in his own strength, he could not. Do you find yourself in this position?

Christians commonly say, "I don't understand why I can't win over temptation. Sin has too powerful a hold on my life."

The second big question is, "When does temptation become a sin?"

The Bull Fight

While reading James Michener's book, *Mexico*, I became intrigued with bullfights. In them, I saw a spiritual illustration.

Every fight includes the bull, the matador, his red cape, and his sword. The bull represents you, the matador is Satan, and his red cape is temptation.

Satan, the matador, waves his red cape of temptation in front of you, the bull. You stomp your feet and kick dirt into the air. Definitely, you snort a few times. Finally, the lure of the cape is too much. You charge.

Satan does not make you charge. You do it of your own free will. You decide to take the bait.

When you vainly attack the red cape of temptation, the devil takes advantage of your charge and stabs you through the heart with his sword.

All sin leads to the death of something. It may be the death of your peace, joy, victory, and power. Sin is an issue which must be dealt with honestly if you really want God to use you in a powerful way.

For example, how does any person find himself or herself on the road to moral impurity? Does a man awaken one morning and say, "Today, I'm going to be unfaithful to my wife. I'm going to commit adultery"?

No. Moral impurity begins in the mind.

Proverbs 4:23 says, "Watch over your heart with all diligence, for from it flow the springs of life."

In *The Living Bible*, this is translated: "Above all else, guard your affections. For they influence everything else in your life."

In *The Living Bible*, Proverbs 23:19 says, "Be wise and stay in God's paths."

In *The Amplified Bible*, it reads, "Direct your mind in the way [of the Lord]."

Every temptation begins in your mind. The battle is won or lost in your mind.

Whenever someone goes astray, it always starts with his or her thought life. People who mess up their lives do not begin with action. They begin with wrong thinking.

Your thoughts determine your actions. Before you can change your actions, you must change your thought life.

For example, immoral sexual relations do not just happen. Long before the actual act, the cultivation of an immoral thought life begins.

In 2 Timothy 2:22, Paul admonished young Timothy to "flee from youthful lusts."

If you want to manage your mind, learn to flee. When you are tempted with lustful thoughts, make a decision to run.

In *The Living Bible*, the above verse reads: "Run from anything that gives you the evil thoughts that young men often have, but stay close to anything that makes you want to do right." A choice accompanies every temptation. Temptation is not sin, but a wrong response to temptation leads to sin. Again, the battle is won or lost in your thought life.

As I write this book, I am in the process of losing 30 pounds. Every day someone sets before me something that is not on my program. Recently, I was eating in a restaurant and doing well. Then the server said, "Your meal includes ice cream."

Ouch! I love ice cream, especially vanilla ice cream with chocolate topping!

How did I resist this temptation? Did I look at it and say, "Just one bite?"

No. The secret to overcoming any temptation is to run away from it. I had to set my mind on something else. This was difficult with the ice cream so close at hand, but I fixed my mind on my goal (my target). With my mind on something besides the ice cream, I was able to escape that temptation.

Falling into the temptation always brings regret, suffering, and defeat.

My dad once told me, "Son, the grass is not greener on the other side of the fence."

He was right. The grass is not greener on the other side of the fence. It is greener where you water it!

Water your mind with clean and pure thoughts. Know your weaknesses. Find Scripture verses that deal with those specific weaknesses. Each time you are tempted in one of these areas, quote those Scriptures that apply.

Waging War

Paul described our struggle with temptation as "waging war." In Romans 7:23, he wrote, "I see a different law in the members of my body, waging war against the law of my mind and making me a prisoner of the law of sin which is in my members."

Finally, in Romans 7:24, he cried, "Wretched man that I am!"

"Wretched" means that he has reached the place of thorough exhaustion, as if he had been doing hard physical labor. In his letter to the Galatian churches, he likened it to a battle: "For the flesh sets its desire against the Spirit, and the Spirit against the flesh; for these are in opposition to one another, so that you may not do the things that you please" (Gal. 5:17).

We see this in the conflict between two men in a boxing ring. They slug it out. Each tries to break through the defenses of the other to land the crippling blow.

In the seventh chapter of Paul's letter to the Romans, the words *Holy Spirit* do not appear. Yet, the word *law* appears more than 20 times. The words *I*, *me*, and *my* occur more than 40 times. In these verses, we have a picture of a Christian struggling to win, through his own self-effort, the battle over temptation and sin.

God allows you to struggle for one reason. He wants to bring you to the end of yourself.

Before you can know Christ as Lord, you must arrive at a state in which you are ready to admit that of yourself, you are

totally helpless. Then you will cry, as Paul did, "Wretched
man that I am!"

TEN

On the Roof Top

Immediately after I preached in a Washington, D.C., church a sermon on "Secret Sin", a woman walked to the platform and asked the senior pastor if she could speak to the church. She was the director of the youth department and was the church's music director. Of course, the pastor allowed her to share.

She began by saying, "I have a secret sin to confess this morning."

Then she stunned the congregation by declaring, "I am committing adultery with one of our deacons."

Wow! What a bombshell!

All the deacons turned to one another and said in unison, "Not me."

Personally, I do not think she should have dealt with this in a public forum, but she did. The cat was out of the bag. The woman, her family, the accused deacon, his family, and the church had to deal with the issue. Suddenly, the public confession of the sin hovered like a dark cloud over all, including innocent bystanders, who heard it.

The principle here is that one's confession should be as public as the sin—meaning that only to those who have knowledge of the sin would one need to confess and ask forgiveness. David teaches us the process of renewing our relationship with God after we have sinned.

Secret Sin

We are all born as sinners. We also choose to disobey
God. We are sinners by nature and by choice.

When Christ enters our hearts, our sins are forgiven.
However, the possibility of secret sins in our lives continues
to exist.

In the Old Testament, in 2 Samuel 11, you can read a tragic story about a godly man, King David. He knew God and
had walked on His path, but he committed two great sins.

One day he looked out from his rooftop and saw a beautiful woman—Bathsheba. She was bathing on her rooftop.
Instead of turning away, David continued to look on her
nakedness. His lust culminated in the sin of adultery.

When Bathsheba became pregnant, David sought to hide
his sin from her husband, Uriah. He brought this loyal soldier
home from active duty and enticed him to sleep with his wife.

Bound by duty to his God and his king, Uriah protested,
"The ark and Israel and Judah are staying in temporary shel-
ters, and my lord Joab and the servants of my lord are camp-
ing in the open field. Shall I then go to my house to eat and to
drink and to lie with my wife? By your life and the life of
your soul, I will not do this thing" (2 Sam. 11:11).

David then ordered Bathsheba's husband sent into the
front lines of a fierce battle, where he was sure to be killed.

The king's sins of adultery and murder were hidden from
people but not from God. 2 Samuel 11:27 says, "The thing
that David had done was evil in the sight of the Lord."

Broken by his sin and its consequences, David cried out in
confession and repentance. His prayer is found in Psalm 51:1-
17:

"Be gracious to me, O God, according to Your lovingkind-
ness;

According to the greatness of Your compassion blot out
my transgressions.

Wash me thoroughly from my iniquity,

And cleanse me from my sin.
For I know my transgressions,
And my sin is ever before me.
Against You, You only, I have sinned
And done what is evil in Your sight,
So that You are justified when You speak
And blameless when You judge.
Behold, I was brought forth in iniquity,
And in sin my mother conceived me.
 Behold, You desire truth in the innermost being,
And in the hidden part You will make me know wisdom.
Purify me with hyssop, and I shall be clean
Wash me, and I shall be whiter than snow.
Make me to hear joy and gladness,
Let the bones which You have broken rejoice.
Hide Your face from my sins
And blot out all my iniquities.
Create in me a clean heart, O God,
And renew a steadfast spirit within me.
Do not cast me away from Your presence
And do not take Your Holy Spirit from me.
Restore to me the joy of Your salvation
And sustain me with a willing spirit.
Then I will teach transgressors Your ways,
And sinners will be converted to You.
Deliver me from blood guiltiness, O God, the God of
     my salvation;
Then my tongue will joyfully sing of Your righteousness.
O Lord, open my lips,
That my mouth may declare Your praise.
For You do not delight in sacrifice, otherwise I would
     give it;
You are not pleased with burnt offering.
The sacrifices of God are a broken spirit;
A broken and a contrite heart, O God, You will not
     despise."

From this prayer, you can learn how to put your own feet back on God's path. David acknowledged his sin and took full responsibility for it. Every part of that confession is important. Seeing your problem is not enough. Just as David did, ask for forgiveness.

When asking for forgiveness David uses three words to describe his sin. Notice the verbs he used as he cried out for forgiveness.

Transgression

The king confessed that he had committed transgressions. In verse one he pleaded for God to "blot out my transgressions."

In Hebrew, *pasha*, which is translated as transgressions, means "deliberate disobedience."

David's sin was no accident. He knew that he was doing wrong. He knew the commandments that forbid adultery and murder. He willfully stepped outside the boundaries and broke God's law. He was without excuse.

David's cry was for God to blot out his transgressions. The verb that is translated "to blot out" means "to cleanse."[1]

This is the same word that is used in Genesis 7:22-23 when the Bible says that, except for Noah and his family, God *destroyed* (*blotted out*) every person in the flood. Every creature that was outside the safety of the ark was eliminated from existence.

King David begged God both to forgive him and to forget his sin. He was asking for the complete elimination of this sin from his life. This is what occurs when you repent of your sin and trust Christ as savior.

In Isaiah 43:25, God says, "I, even I, am the one who wipes out your transgressions for My own sake; And I will not remember your sins."

David's sin was like a debt written down in God's book. It needed to be blotted out. He asked God not just to mark through the record, so that no one could read it. He asked that it be so eliminated that no trace of it remained.

When my children were young, one very popular toy was called the "Magic Slate." It is a piece of black cardboard covered with a sheet of translucent plastic. A child writes and draws on it with a wooden stylus, but when the plastic sheet is pulled up, all the marks disappear. The slate is clean.

You cannot magically erase all the ugly marks of sin on your record, but God can.

Iniquity

David also used in his confession a second word for sin: *iniquity*. This springs from the Hebrew word *awon*, which means crookedness.

Imagine that a man builds a wall, which all the people in his village admire. They tell him, "You are a good mason—the best in these parts. Your wall is straight—the straightest in the village."

Then, one day a master mason visits the village, looks at the wall, and says, "I do not believe that is straight."

While the proud local mason and all his fellow villagers watch, the visitor pulls out a plumb (a small mass of lead suspended by a line of thread). He holds it up against the wall. To everyone's amazement, against that perfectly straight plumb line, the wall is shown to be crooked.

King David had been full of self-righteous pride. He probably reasoned, "I'm not perfect, but I am a good man. I go to temple regularly and offer sacrifices. I am a good father and an honest businessperson. Compared to other people, I measure up pretty well."

Then the day arrived when God dropped His plumb line alongside David's life. He sent His prophet, Nathan, to the king with a story of a great injustice. He said, "There were two men in one city, the one rich and the other poor. The rich man had a great many flocks and herds. But the poor man had nothing except one little ewe lamb which he bought and nourished; and it grew up together with him and his children. It would eat of his bread and drink of his cup and lie in his bosom, and was like a daughter to him. Now a traveler came to the rich man, and he was unwilling to take from his own flock or his own herd, to prepare for the wayfarer who had come to him; rather he took the poor man's ewe lamb and prepared it for the man who had come to him" (2 Sam. 12:1-4).

When David heard this, he lashed out against the rich man saying, "As the Lord lives, surely the man who has done this deserves to die. He must make restitution for the lamb fourfold, because he did this thing and had no compassion" (vv. 5-6).

At this point the blow fell. The prophet confronted the king with these words, "You are the man! Thus says the Lord God of Israel, 'It is I who anointed you king over Israel and it is I who delivered you from the hand of Saul. I also gave you your master's house and your master's wives into your care, and I gave you the house of Israel and Judah; and if that had been too little, I would have added to you many more things like these! Why have you despised the word of the Lord by doing evil in His sight? You have struck down Uriah the Hittite with the sword, have taken his wife to be your wife, and have killed him with the sword of the sons of Ammon'" (vv. 7-9).

David's sin was exposed. He had to see himself as guilty: a lawbreaker, off the path, and out of God's will. Broken, he pleaded, "Wash me thoroughly from my iniquity" (Psalm 51:2).

It is translated here as "wash thoroughly." This verb occurs 51 times in the Old Testament. It literally means "to purify."[2] It usually refers to people or priests who appeared before God with clean clothes during a religious ceremony. This was ordered in Exodus 19:10-11, "The Lord also said to Moses, 'Go to the people and consecrate them today and tomorrow, and let them wash their garments; and let them be ready for the third day, for on the third day the Lord will come down on Mount Sinai in the sight of all the people.'"

So that they could be set apart (holy) before God, people would soak their clothes in cold water, beat them on a large rock, and stomp on them until they were completely clean and pure. David wanted to be as consecrated to the Lord as his clothes were clean after being thoroughly washed.

His sin was like deeply ingrained dirt which needed to be removed.

As a boy, David's shepherd's tunic had often gotten soaked with blood from the thorn-torn side of a lamb he had rescued from a thicket. It had been stained with the mud of a pit from which he had dragged a straying sheep. He had watched as his mother had soaked his dirty tunic in a cold stream. She had then slapped, beat, and rubbed until that garment was clean.

Now the king asked God to do for him what his mother had done for his dirty clothes. He was saying, "I am stained with the filth of sin. I feel so dirty! Lord, make every fiber of my soul clean."

Sin

The third Hebrew word David uses to describe what he had done is *hatah*. In Psalm 51:3, it is translated as sin ("my sin is ever before me"). This means "to miss the mark."

When he was a young man, David learned to use a sling-shot. No doubt, when he attempted to hit a target and failed, one of his friends shouted, "See, you missed the target again."

As a man guilty of great sin, David might have cried, as he remembered this: "Oh, God, you made me for higher things than adultery, drunkenness, and murder. How I have missed the mark!"

If you would really confess your sin, you must be willing to say with King David, "My sin is truly sinful. I have missed the mark." You have not truthfully confessed and begun to live as a 24/7 Christian until you have accepted full responsibility for your sin. You must agree with God that you are guilty and without any excuse.

In Psalm 51:2, David uses the verb *cleanse*. He pleads with God, "Cleanse me from my sin."

This verb means "to be pure or to be pronounced innocent." In the New Testament, the word has the idea of being innocent or without guilt.[3] David was asking God to treat him as if he was innocent, without any guilt.

David's sin was like leprosy from which he needed cleansing. In ancient times, a person who contracted leprosy was cut off by the law from friends and family. That person could not stay in the city or live at home. When anyone approached, he or she had to cry out the warning, "Unclean! Unclean!"

But once a person was healed of this dread disease, that one could go to a priest, who would examine him or her and certify that the leper was clean. David pleaded, "Lord, I feel like leprosy has gotten inside me. I am sick with my sin. Cleanse and heal me; I pray!"

Accepting responsibility for your sin is never easy. The inclination is often to blame someone else. Adam and Eve invented the game of "pass the buck." Since then, every member of the race has become an expert at excusing himself by blaming someone else.

David may have been tempted to shift the blame to Bathsheba. Instead, he took full responsibility for what he had done. He had committed both adultery and murder. He was guilty. He had gotten off God's path. Now, he was facing his sin with confession and repentance.

Psalm 51:4 reveals David's profound recognition that his sin was not only against other people but also against God. He acknowledged, "Against Thee, Thee only, I have sinned and done what is evil in Thy sight, so that Thou are justified when Thou dost speak and blameless when Thou dost judge."

From the story of King David, one learns that if Satan can tempt such a strong and godly person to fall into secret sin, he can also entice anyone to do the same.[4]

[1]Benjanin Davidson, *The Analytical Hebrew and Chaldea Lexicon* (Grand Rapids: Zondervan, 1977), 478.

[2]Spiros Zodhiates, *The Hebrew-Greek Key Study Bible* (Chattanooga: AMG Publishers, 1984), 1065.

[3]*Greek English Dictionary of the New Testament* (New York: United Bible Societies, 1971), 246.

[4]I am indebted to Dr. Cecil R. Taylor, Dean of Department of Religion of the University of Mobile, Alabama, for teaching me these principles from Psalm 51 regarding sin and for supplying me with his research on this subject.

ELEVEN

Struggles We Face

You have read far enough by now to know that I do not pull any punches about the struggles you will face as a disciple of Christ. Experience has taught me that four struggles are paramount: doubt, deep anger, guilt and bitterness.

Doubt

One of my earliest memories is that of telling my first-grade school teacher that I had accepted Jesus as my personal Lord and Savior. The previous day, Miss Minnie, my Sunday-school teacher, had led me to Christ. My mother recalls how this godly woman emerged from her Sunday-school classroom to announce to my mother that I had given my life to the Lord. My mother also remembers my making the same confession to her.

To this day, I do not remember the exact moment when I received Christ. All I remember is telling my first-grade teacher the next day at school. Later in life, I began to wonder what really happened.

Once I heard an evangelist say, "If you cannot remember the exact moment of your conversion, then you are not saved." In spite of this, I knew Christ was in my life. Without any doubt, I believed in my heart that Jesus was my Savior. I confessed Him as such.

When I was seven, I was baptized. During my formative years, I had a deep hunger to know more of Christ and to learn as much as I could about the Word of God.

My heart was also burdened for lost people. I remember standing in my front yard and shouting John 3:16 as loudly as I could. I listened to my voice echoing across the woods. I hoped someone on the other side would hear and be saved. Another time I went to a man who stood on a ladder as he worked on a neighbor's house. I began preaching to him. He was so shocked that he almost fell.

Even though I manifested every evidence of a transformed life, when I heard that evangelist say that I was lost if I could not remember the moment of my conversion, fear and doubt began to seize my mind and heart. I tried to reconstruct what had happened in that Sunday-school classroom when I was six. I could not do it. I could not remember any of the details. All I could remember was confessing Christ to my first-grade school teacher. I could not recall the moment when I crossed the line.

In spite of knowing on what I call "a gut-level number nine" that I had trusted Jesus as Lord and Savior, I began to doubt. In spite of the fact that when I was 15, I had totally surrendered to Him as Lord, the doubts persisted. It was all because I could not remember the exact moment when, as a six-year-old child, I crossed the line between being saved and being lost.

One day I was really troubled by this. So I went home, got on my knees, buried my head in our living room couch, and prayed this prayer: "Lord, if I messed up as a child and did not do it right, right now I am trusting you." At that moment a peace fell over me. God assured me that Jesus was in my life and I was safe in His arms. That was like driving down a stake.

Over the years, I have discovered that this type of experience is common among those of us who had childhood conversions or who were reared in Christian families. This is why so many of us have a later, deep, committal experience regarding the lordship of Christ. I believe this is our entering into a deeper understanding of faith and commitment, but it is almost like a second conversion. A believer can be justified only once, but experiences can take us deeper into our relationship with Christ. The primary thing is to know that you have acknowledged Jesus as the Lord of your life.

We must cross a line from death to life, from being lost to being saved. Still, I have met many deeply committed Christians, even preachers of the gospel, who confess that they have difficulty recalling and defining the exact moment of their conversion.

One dear, missionary friend shares in his testimony that, while in the U.S. Navy, he was driving his car while he was drunk. He hit another car. Instead of getting angry, the car's owner invited him to a Bible study. Out of obligation he went to the study. Three weeks later, at a Baptist church in Taiwan, he and his wife made public professions of their faith in Christ. Later, he looked back and wondered, "When did I actually cross the line?"

"I do not know," he says. "I just know that one day I was a drunken sailor. Three weeks later, I was professing Christ as the Lord of my life."

Another personal friend who is an evangelist and has had a tremendous impact on my life and ministry has almost the exact same experience as I had. I do not know of any evangelist in the world that has preached to more people on the actual front lines in the streets of the world than this man of God. Yet, he was reared in a home where the gospel was not taught or preached. As a child he heard his grandmother teach him about the gospel. He said as he read the Word of God, a light came on. Later, when he was a highly successful airline pilot, God called him to preach the gospel to the lost of the world. He surrendered his life totally to the Lord, quit his job, and went to Bible college to prepare for the ministry. Today, he has literally touched hundreds of thousands of lives "for the sake of the gospel", as he would say. Yet, as he looks back at exactly when he actually crossed the conversion line he just simply says, "God knows, and that is all that matters."

Satan still tries to attack me in my mind, accusing me for not remembering the exact moment of my conversion. He will do anything to create doubt. In my case, he tries to use logic. I have learned that one can not overcome his attacks by mere reasoning. In Isaiah 55:8 the Bible says, "'For My thoughts are not your thoughts, neither are your ways My ways,' declares the Lord."

Being born into God's family through His unmerited love (grace) is a mystery. For some people, the salvation experience is highly emotional. In tears they trust Christ. Others experience no emotional expression. Some trust Christ with great belief. Others trust with faith the size of a mustard seed (Matt. 17:20). The important thing is trusting Him.

Jesus said, "The one who comes to Me I will certainly not cast out" (John 6:37b).

If doubts occur, don't seek a unique feeling or a sign from Heaven. In simple, childlike faith, take God at His word. Believe Him.

Personally, I told the Lord that I do not desire a special sign. I do not even want to depend on a memory. Even on a deeper level, I do not even want to put my faith in my faith. Faith does not save. Jesus saves. I simply want to walk by pure faith in Christ. Both the Holy Spirit and God's Word (the Bible) confirm my salvation. He lives in my heart; that is all I need to know. 1 John 5:12 (NIV) says, "He who has the Son has life; he who does not have the Son of God does not have life."

If this is ever an issue with you, then ask the Holy Spirit to quietly speak to you, revealing your true state before Him. He will speak. When He does, obey Him. If He tells you that you need to receive Christ as your personal Lord and Savior, immediately invite Christ into your life. If He tells you that Christ is in your life already, stand on that ground by faith. When Satan attacks, continue standing on that ground.

Your basis for assurance of salvation is threefold: the Holy Spirit within you, the promises in the Word of God, and the transformed life.

1. Regarding the Holy Spirit, God's Word says:

Romans 8:11 (NIV): "And if the Spirit of him who raised Jesus from the dead is living in you, he who raised Christ from the dead will also give life to your mortal bodies through his Spirit, who lives in you."

Romans 8:16 (NIV): "The Spirit himself testifies with our spirit that we are God's children."

2. Regarding God's Word, God gives us the following promises:

John 1:12 (NIV): "Yet to all who received him, to those who believed in his name, he gave the right to become children of God."

Romans 8:1 (NIV): "Therefore, there is now no condemnation for those who are in Christ Jesus."

2 Corinthians 1: 21b-22 (NIV): "He anointed us, set his seal of ownership on us, and put his Spirit in our hearts as a deposit, guaranteeing what is to come."

2 Corinthians 7:10 (NIV): "Godly sorrow brings repentance that leads to salvation and leaves no regret, but worldly sorrow brings death."

Galatians 2:20 (NIV): "I have been crucified with Christ and I no longer live, but Christ lives in me. The life I live in the body, I live by faith in the Son of God, who loved me and gave himself for me."

Ephesians 1:13b-14 (NIV): "Having believed, you were marked in him with a seal, the promised Holy Spirit, who is a deposit guaranteeing our inheritance until the redemption of those who are God's possession—to the praise of his glory."

Colossians 1:27 (NIV): "Christ in you, the hope of Glory."

1 John 5:12 (NIV) says, "He who has the Son has life; he who does not have the Son of God does not have life."

3. The transformed life. I have never doubted that Jesus Christ has entered my life and radically changed my life. When I was age six, He radically changed me the first time. He changed the direction of my life from the direction I would have taken in life. He radically transformed my life again at age 15 when, as a teen-ager, I totally surrendered to him again in a deepening lordship experience.

The question for you as you read this book is this: Ask yourself, has Jesus Christ changed my life? Does He really and truly live within my life? Does His Spirit testify with my spirit that I am a child of God? Do I have the peace of God that when I die I will go to heaven?

If not or if you are unsure, as I was, then drive down a stake before you continue to read this book. Just simply pray a prayer directly to Jesus Christ right now and invite him into your heart as both Lord and Savior. Ask him to forgive you of your sins and take full control of your life from this point on. Drive down your stake for all eternity.

Deep Anger

Thinking about the struggle of deep anger, I recall the time when I was still in the horrible grip of the pain and darkness of grief over Sherry's death three months earlier. I was just trying to survive day by day. Then my mother called from Monroe, Louisiana, to my home in Belo Horizonte to tell me that my father might not survive the surgery he had just undergone. Immediately, I rushed to the airport and arrived, just before he died, at the bedside of this man that I loved dearly.

After my father's funeral, I returned to Belo Horizonte as soon as possible, because now I was a single parent, the high-school Homeschool teacher of my youngest son, Jason, and a missionary. My weeks were filled with teaching Jason in the mornings, doing missionary work in the afternoons and evenings, and traveling on weekends to preach.

Just one week after I returned from my dad's funeral, I spoke at a weekend conference in a small town called Manhuacu. In the evenings, I preached about revival and spiritual awakening. All day on Saturday I did Pioneer Evangelism training. During every session, the church was packed with people.

I had experienced a glorious weekend of ministry, but as I drove back to Belo Horizonte on Sunday afternoon, I was thinking about how I had to get ready to teach my son the next day his lessons for his senior year in high school. Work and home responsibilities, bonded with the overwhelming sense of grief, were threatening to wear me down.

I arrived late that afternoon. Jason, my son, had already left for the evening service at our church. I opened the door of an empty house. For the first time in 23 years, I had returned home with no one there to greet me. Always before, Sherry had been there. I would see her radiant smile and feel the warm welcome of her kiss. This time, no one was there. The horrible reality of that struck me as though I had been hit with a powerful and angry fist.

In my bedroom, I threw myself on the bed and cried. I pounded the pillows with my fists, kicked my legs in a fury, and screamed out of loneliness and pain. Within three months, I had lost my wife and father. I was angry with God for allowing all of this to happen to me. I cried until I was exhausted.

Finally, when I was emptied and had no more tears to cry, I picked up my Bible and began to read. In the past, God had always spoken to me through his Word. That night I needed desperately to hear from Him. I was not disappointed. I came upon these words in Isaiah 43:2, "When you walk through the fire, you shall not be burned" (NKJV).

I experienced the Holy Spirit speaking to me in a loud, audible voice. Here I was in the middle of a fire hotter and more threatening than anything I had ever encountered—the biggest firestorm of my life. How could I possibly survive? God was telling me that He would not save me from the fire, but He would save me in the fire. He was saying, "You will walk through the fire, but you will not get burned."

That night, I lay back on my bed, took in what my Lord was saying to me, and knew that I was going to make it. From that moment, I knew I would survive and live again. Yes, I was in the fire, but God was not going to allow me to get burned. He had spoken. This was the beginning of hope. I knew that I was going to make it through the fire.

Many live today with deep anger in their hearts. Maybe you have experienced a great loss, or you have suffered an injustice. You feel paralyzed with grief. You believe that you can't go on. Unresolved, this can be as devastating as bitterness. I have been there. I have discovered that our Lord is also the Way out of debilitating anger. Whatever you are going through, He has not forsaken you. When you find yourself in this state, turn to God's Word. God has a word from His Word to both comfort and deliver you.

Guilt

Guilt is another battlefield on which sin can confront and defeat you.

Because God created us with a conscience, guilt is a part of our being. We can be thankful for this. Problems arise when we fail to recognize that two kinds of guilt exist—that which is real and that which is false.

June Hunt, the voice of Hope for the Heart radio ministry, says, "False guilt is based on feelings. There can be no confession with false guilt. False guilt occurs when you blame yourself when you have committed no wrong."[1]

June Hunt explains that Satan loves to burden believers with false guilt. He will bring up sins from your past life, before you gave your life to Jesus. He will try to make you feel guilty once again for sin that has already been confessed and forgiven by God. You may keep asking God to forgive you of the same sin over and over again. When this occurs, you are experiencing the devil's accusations.

If you are experiencing false guilt, no amount of confession will bring relief. The sense of guilt will keep appearing over and over.

False guilt will blame, condemn, and bring shame on a person when, in reality, the individual is not guilty, especially after he or she has confessed and repented of the wrong done in the past. Recognize false guilt as a lie from hell.

On the other hand, guilt which is real also occurs. True guilt is felt when real sin has been committed. King David was guilty of real sins when he committed adultery and murder.

June Hunt says that conviction of sin comes from two sources—a natural, God-given conscience and the Spirit of God.[2]

You will feel true guilt when the Holy Spirit convicts you of sin. He wants to lead you to confession and repentance, so that you can experience forgiveness. If you allow Him to do so, God will use guilt to change you.

Jesus said, "But when He, the Spirit of truth, comes, He will guide you into all the truth; for He will not speak on His own initiative, but whatever He hears, He will speak; and He will disclose to you what is to come. He shall glorify Me, for He shall take of Mine and shall disclose it to you" (John 16:13).

You can have the confidence that the Holy Spirit will guide your conscience by speaking truth into your heart.

Bitterness

Bitterness is a sin that has the potential of destroying your whole life. It reaches beyond you and affects your family and friends. It will poison your whole sphere of influence.

Hebrews 12:14-15 warns us to "Pursue peace with all men, and the sanctification without which no one will see the

Lord. See to it that no one comes short of the grace of God; that no root of bitterness springing up causes trouble, and by it many be defiled."

Every so often, missionaries are allowed to return to the United States to minister and report to the churches that support them. As part of my Stateside assignments I often preach during spiritual-awakening conferences in local churches. On one of these occasions, I spoke on the subject of anger and bitterness. Afterward, a woman told me her tragic story.

She had been reared in the home of a minister. Every Sunday she was taken to church and heard her father preach, but he had a dark side. Her father was sexually abusing his daughter.

For many years the woman had carried this anger and bitterness deep inside of her. Her bitterness was a natural response, but she needed to be healed of this soul wound in order to have victory and to experience the abundant life which Jesus promised.

I prayed, asking God what I should say to her. He led me to ask, "Are you a Christian? Have you given your life to Christ?"

"Yes", she replied.

Then, I asked, "Do you recall one of the last things Jesus said as He was dying on the cross?"

She answered, "He said, 'Father, forgive them for they do not know what they are doing.'"

"You, in and of yourself, do not have the capacity to forgive your father," I told her "But, Jesus in you does.

"Jesus loves all people, regardless of what sin they may have committed against Him," I continued. "After what your father did to you, of yourself, you do not have the capacity to love him. But, if you want to be delivered from this bondage of hate and bitterness, allow Jesus inside of you to both love and forgive him."

She understood. That night she prayed like this: "Lord, I cannot forgive my dad, but you can. So, in the name of Jesus,

I forgive him. I cannot love my dad, but Jesus, you can. So, I declare that I love him in Jesus name."

That night she was delivered from the bondage of bitterness. She sensed a relief she had not experienced in her entire life.

[1]June Hunt, *God's Heart on . . . Guilt* (Dallas: Hope for the Heart, 2000), 10.
[2]Ibid., 37.

TWELVE

Lessons from the Practice Field

Have you ever just wanted to give up? Oh, how Satan wants you to do just that!

Every child of God deals with defeat and discouragement. One of Satan's most effective strategies is to discourage you, tempt you to quit, and drive you into depression.

August does not produce weather in north Louisiana that is designed for playing football, but in August 1964, our Bastrop high school team regularly dressed in full pads and helmets for our two-and-one-half hour practice. The heat and humidity were suffocating. Our tough coach rarely relented and allowed anyone to drink water.

I remember very specifically one of those afternoons. We had run, hit, blocked, and tackled until I was on the brink of total collapse. Big linemen were in tears due to the heat and physical exhaustion. That day, I literally thought that I was going to die.

Finally, I said to myself, "I'm quitting. I can't take this any longer."

Then I heard an inner voice say, "If you quit now, some-day on the mission field when the going gets tough, you will quit again."

At that point, I had never thought about being a missionary, but I knew that the Holy Spirit was speaking those words to my heart. I heard and remembered what He told me on that brutal practice field.

Twenty-five years later, I was on the mission field in Brazil. My youngest son, Jason, and I had traveled for hours on a rough, unpaved road. The weather was hot; we had been eating dust all day. Finally, we arrived at a small city in the interior of the state of Minas Gerais. We were there to show a film about the life, crucifixion, and resurrection of Jesus, and to preach the gospel in the city's central plaza.

To publicize the event and gather a crowd, I had to drive around the town for several hours announcing the program through a special sound system and speakers that I had attached to the top of my car After finishing the promotion, I still had to set up all the equipment for the event. My son and I spent almost two hours positioning the speakers, connecting the wiring, erecting the screen for the film, putting up an easel for a special illustrated message, preparing the black light and fluorescent paints, and setting up the projector.

The day had been long and tiring; but when night fell, the reward for the day's work occurred. People arrived from all directions and filled the central plaza. Soon, it was packed with over 1,500 men, women, boys, and girls. None were sitting. Everyone stood to watch the film and listen to the illustrated message.

Five minutes into the film a five-cent fuse blew out and knocked out all the lights, our projector, and the sound system. The people could not possibly hear anything. With a broken heart, I had to stand on top of our truck and say, "You can go home. We have no sound."

This was too much. I had never experienced anything like the exhaustion and defeat that I felt that night. As the crowd walked away, I lay down on top of the truck, looked up into the thousands of stars filling the sky over Brazil, and became consumed with despair.

Lying there, I prayed a prayer I had never prayed before: "Lord, I quit. I can't keep doing this. I quit."

Quitting is not in my nature. It is not a part of me. I have never been a quitter, but that night I could take no more. Day after day and night after night, I faithfully preached the gospel, but that night I had run out of gas. I was exhausted, frustrated, and angry. I was ready to quit.

Lying flat on my back, on top of our truck, I again heard God speak to me. He spoke with a still, small voice such as the one with which He spoke to Elijah. He said, "Wade, get up. You are not going to quit. Now, put up your equipment."

At that stage of my missionary career, I had a lot to learn. I had already been taught one of life's most important lessons on a sun-baked football practice field in Louisiana. If I was to be really effective, it would be because I had gone to the school of hard knocks.

Now, I often remember how God spoke to a teenage football player, who had no idea that he would ever be a missionary. He knew how many times I would have to face days in which the chips were down, and I would feel like quitting. Each time that happens, I hear Him say, "If you quit now, someday on the mission field, when the going gets tough, you will quit again."

Paul, who never quit, had learned by enduring difficulty that he could do all things through Christ who strengthened him (Phil. 4:13).

Only when you have reached the end of yourself and gone on in His strength are you ready to be effective as His servant. Don't quit.

You may be discouraged right now. Maybe the pressures of your work, financial situation, and home life threaten to overwhelm you. Once you had a vision, a dream. Now, you are tempted to give up on that dream. Listen, God is saying something: "Don't quit! Don't give up!"

The Broom Tree

Even Elijah, the prophet, was tempted to give up—to quit. In the Old Testament, in 1 Kings 16-19, you can read the dramatic story of Elijah. He was a godly prophet, but he was not immune to discouragement. Even though he had been called to be God's spokesperson and had witnessed miracles, he found himself dejected and defeated.

King Ahab had married a wicked queen, Jezebel. She introduced the godless worship of Baal into Israel. Elijah confronted the king with this wickedness and prophesied that no more dew or rain would fall until he, himself, said so.

This caused great hardship in Israel. Elijah himself suffered and was kept alive by ravens and the water from a small brook.

When the brook dried up, he found a widow named Zarephath. All she had was a little flour in a jar and a little oil in a jug. When the prophet arrived, she was out gathering sticks for a fire to bake a last meal for herself and her son. They faced starvation.

God performed a miracle. The little jar of flour and the jug of oil did not run dry again until the rain came.

In spite of all this, the woman's son became ill and died. Again, in Elijah's presence, God moved in a miraculous way. The son was brought back to life.

Later, Elijah challenged all of Ahab's prophets to a duel. Four-hundred fifty prophets of Baal faced Elijah. On Mount Carmel, Elijah asked a penetrating question: "How long will you hesitate between two opinions? If the Lord is God, follow Him; but if Baal, follow him" (1 Kings 18:21).

Elijah challenged the prophets of Baal to prepare their altars. They were to slaughter two bulls and place them on the wood on the altar, but they were not to light a fire. Instead, they were to call out to their god. Afterward, Elijah would call out to his God. The true God would send fire to consume the sacrifice.

When the prophets of Baal prayed, nothing happened. Elijah mocked, "Call out with a loud voice, for he is a god; either he is occupied or gone aside, or is on a journey, or perhaps he is asleep and needs to be awakened" (1 Kings 18:27).

They continued to cry out but nothing happened—no voice, no fire, nothing.

When time arrived for the evening sacrifice, Elijah called the onlookers around him. With quiet authority he directed the use of 12 stones to rebuild the altar—one stone for each of the tribes of Israel. Around the altar, he dug a trench, arranged the wood, cut the bull into pieces and laid it on the wood. Then he ordered four large jars to be filled and poured over the sacrifice. This was done three times.

When Elijah cried out to the one true God, fire fell from heaven and consumed the sacrifice. Stunned, the prophets of Baal fell on their faces and cried out, "The Lord, He is God; the Lord, He is God" (1 Kings 18:39).

What a revival! What a spiritual awakening!

Personally, I cannot imagine God using me in such a way. I know that He can, but I have yet to experience anything such as what happened on Mount Carmel. Following that, you would think that Elijah would not be afraid of anyone or anything.

But wait. When Ahab told his wife, Jezebel, what had happened on Mount Carmel, she was furious. She totally lost it. In a rage, she sent a royal messenger to tell Elijah that he was a marked man. She was after him and would not stop until she killed him.

Elijah, the prophet who had seen so many miracles, was afraid. He ran for his life. The Bible says, "But he himself went a day's journey into the wilderness and came and sat down under a lone broom or juniper tree and asked that he might die" (1 Kings 19:4, *The Amplified Bible*).

In the immediate aftermath of his greatest spiritual triumph, the prophet was beaten. He wanted to quit. He was discouraged.

Have you ever found yourself under your own broom tree?

God uses "the struggle" to strengthen our faith. In seeking God to help us overcome sin, our relationship with God is deepened and our faith grows.

James 1:2-4 (NIV) says, "Consider it pure joy, my brothers, whenever you face trials of many kinds, because you know that the testing of your faith develops perseverance. Perseverance must finish its work so that you may be mature and complete, not lacking anything."

Our sin nature will always be a part of our lives this side of glory, but "the waging war" can be won by the divine nature within us. Each time, we arise from the struggle stronger.

THIRTEEN

A Work in Progress

At an early age I was saved. By the time I was 15, I knew, deep down, that God was calling me to preach the gospel, but I was running away from this as fast as I could. My ambition was to be a football coach, not a preacher. At the same time as I was struggling with my life's calling, I also began to pick the wrong friends. I began to use bad language.

One summer night in New Mexico changed everything. My parents had taken me with them to Glorieta Baptist Assembly near Santa Fe. This was to be a week of recreation and Bible study. On the Saturday night of this week-long retreat, I found myself sitting alone on the back row of the conference hall. The preacher finished his message and invited people to step to the altar and give their lives to Christ.

In that moment, the Holy Spirit powerfully convicted me of sin. He showed me just how self-centered my life really was. It hit me strongly. I could hear my heart beating in my eardrums. I was so shaken that I grabbed the pew in front of me and held on for support. I was also holding on to keep myself from going forward. Again, I knew that God was calling me to turn from my sin and to preach the gospel. That night, I knew that He was calling for more. He was asking me to acknowledge Him as Lord and surrender everything to Him.

After I had resisted through what seemed like 50 verses of the old, gospel hymn of "Just as I Am", I thought that the service was finally over. Still, as I prepared to leave, the disturbance in my heart would not go away. While the preacher made some final announcements, I silently prayed, "Lord, if You will let them sing one more verse, I will go to the altar and commit myself to You fully."

As soon as I finished praying, I heard the preacher say, "I feel led of God to sing one more verse."

As they sang another verse, I let go of the pew and took that first step. When I did this, the burden of sin, like a heavyweight, was lifted from me. I felt as light as a feather as I continued the long walk to the altar. I knew that my sins were forgiven. Christ completely took over the control of my life. I was destined to be His messenger—to preach the gospel the rest of my life.

That night in New Mexico, my life was totally and forever transformed. At that altar, I surrendered everything to Jesus— my sins, my life, my future, my future wife, my career, my body, my mind, and my soul. It was an unconditional surrender to His lordship. The Holy Spirit of God consumed me with Himself. I was radically changed. My bad language was instantly gone. My desires in life were immediately changed. I returned to Bastrop and, within three weeks, began preaching.

On that Saturday night, at Glorieta Baptist Assembly, Jesus Christ became absolutely the Lord of my life. He so changed me that I know He is the answer to the deepest problems and issues people have. Jesus is my Savior. He is my Lord. His lordship over my life goes to the core of my being. This fact has determined my past, determines my present, and will determine my future. Jesus is Lord!

Sanctification

As a little boy, when I opened my heart to Jesus, I was justified. Something else also happened. God immediately began the process of sanctification in my life.

Being sanctified can be compared to taking a bath to wash dirt from your body. It is a process by which the Holy Spirit cleans you as a Christian on the inside. It is His work to make you holy (spiritually pure), like Christ.

Just as you are born once, but bathe often, you are justified once and for all of eternity when you turn by faith to Christ as your Lord and Savior, but the process of sanctification is ongoing. From the moment that you are justified, the Holy Spirit begins to operate in your heart in a practical way to make you holy. This is the "working out" of your salvation (Phil. 2:12-13).

You cannot separate justification and sanctification. To be a Christian means that you are justified and that you are being sanctified. If someone asks you if you are saved, you can answer, "Yes, once and forever", because Christ is in your life.

If that person then asks, "Are you sanctified?"

You can tell that individual, "Yes, many times, and many more times will occur, as well."

In 1 Corinthians 6, Paul describes the immorality of the unrighteous who will not inherit the Kingdom of God. Then, in verse 11, he addresses Christians with these words: "Such were some of you; but you were washed, but you were sanctified, but you were justified in the name of the Lord Jesus Christ and in the Spirit of our God."

One Sunday morning, in Springhill, Louisiana, I was justified at the age of six. One night in Glorieta, New Mexico, at the age of 15, the Holy Spirit continued the process of sanctification in my life. Through it, He brought me into the center of God's will for my life. The process continues in my life today. It will continue until I stand in the presence of Christ. Right now, I am a work in progress.

Again, Paul wrote about this in 2 Thessalonians 2:13; "But we should always give thanks to God for you, brethren beloved by the Lord, because God has chosen you from the beginning for salvation through sanctification by the Spirit and faith in the truth."

If you have been justified through repentance and faith in Christ, you can be thankful that the Holy Spirit is at work in your heart, sanctifying you. Through this process, He wants to bring you to a place of full, absolute, total surrender. This will position you for God to use you to make an awesome difference in your world.

God's School of Brokenness

Along the road of sanctification God takes us through times of brokenness. This as well as "the struggle with sins" is used to mold us in the hands of God to become that which He can use for His honor and glory.

Deciding what I was going to do with my life was not a big problem. While I was still in high school, I knew that God had called me to preach the gospel.

Preparation was the only real issue that I faced. This meant going to college and seminary.

In college, I studied sociology. I learned about every facet of modern social issues. Finishing on a fast track—in three years—was a major feat for an average student such as I was.

Without any break, I plunged into my seminary work. For the next three years, I was buried in the studies of theology, pastoral ministries, Greek and Hebrew. When I finished this six-year marathon, I was burned out but prepared for the work to which God had called me.

During my final year of seminary studies, I heard that the Foreign Mission Board (now International Mission Board) of the Southern Baptist Convention was seeking an evangelist willing to go to South Vietnam, at the height of the war there. Believing that God was leading me to respond, I volunteered.

Soon, I was to learn that even though I had been through the 18 long years of formal educational preparation, I had one more school to attend. This time, I would have no human professors. I would have no books to read, no papers to write, and no Greek words to memorize. I would not have to memorize all those kings in the books of 1 and 2 Kings of the Old Testament. I would not have to stay up all night studying for an exam. In this school, the classes would be different. I would major in brokenness.

Before God can use a person, He must first break that person. The chief hindrance in total surrender to Christ is the middle letter of the word *sin*, "I."

Going to Vietnam, I had a lot of pride and a giant ego. After all, I had finished college and seminary. Now, I was ready to show the world what "I" could do for God.

Knowing me better than I knew myself, God gave me a quick start in His school. I was sent to Ba Ngoi, a little village on the coast of Central South Vietnam, just south of Cam Ranh Bay Air Force Base. For a month, I was to live near my supervisor, Walter Routh, and learn some basic Vietnamese.

I was quartered in a French hotel. However, no illusions of grandeur existed about the place. Every night I slept under mosquito netting. The hotel had no electricity, so I had to use a lantern to write and study. Before going to bed, I would place my pants over the back of a chair. I remember one night specifically because on this particular occasion I had accidentally allowed one of the pants legs to touch the floor. The next morning I pulled on my pants, and a rat ran out of that leg.

Each morning, a local man arrived to tutor me. We sat for four hours repeating Vietnamese tones over and over. Their language has five different tones. I had to learn all of them. By the end of the month, I knew the tones and had mastered a few phrases.

Because of bad drinking water, I became terribly sick. I was vomiting and had diarrhea at the same time. I was extremely weak and could not keep anything in my stomach.

One night I heard an American soldier and a prostitute shouting at one another next door. I went to their room and told them that I was very sick. I said that if they heard me screaming, to please not come in and shoot me.

Later that evening, a lady with black teeth showed up at my door. The couple I had disturbed had walked for hours into the forest to find this woman. She was a nurse. The prostitute could speak English. She explained that the nurse had arrived to give me a shot. It was going to help me. Then, the nurse said, "Take off your pants and bend over."

Too weak to protest, I obeyed. She stuck me with a long needle and injected something into me. To this day, I have no idea what it was. The next morning I was better.

While in Vietnam, I contracted an ameba that was not discovered until three years after I returned to the United States. This caused a radical weight loss.

Following my brief language study, my supervisor took me to the fourth-largest city in South Vietnam—Nha Trang. It sits on one of the most beautiful beaches in the world.

Arrangements were made for me to stay in a small and very rustic apartment. Everything about the place was small, including the bed. It was held up by food cans and draped with a mosquito net. A Vietnamese woman, who could not speak English, was hired to cook for me. We communicated by using an English-Vietnamese dictionary.

After one week, the cook showed me the dictionary. She ran her finger down one side of a page until she found her word. Then she moved her finger across to the English word. I read it three times. I had to make sure I understood what she was telling me. No mistake was made; it read, "I quit."

At this point I stopped and realized my situation. Here I was in a large city—alone and sick. My only means of survival—my Vietnamese cook—was quitting. All of the Greek in the world was not going to help me now. I found myself on rock-bottom. I was totally broken. I got on my knees and wept before God. I cried out that I was sorry for how I had felt. I was sorry for convincing myself that I was a big-shot, missionary evangelist.

I can see now God was showing me a radically important fundamental for life. Until I emptied myself and became nothing, so He could become everything in my life, He could not use me.

In Nha Trang is a huge statue of Buddha. It sits on a hill and overlooks the city. One day, after God had broken me, I climbed that hill and saw the crowd of people gathered there. They were praying, offering incense, and chanting to a god who could not hear, could not touch, could not feel, could not love, could not forgive sins, and who could not save. I turned and looked out over the city of Nha Trang and cried out to God, "Use me to bring your message to this city."

Millions of Vietnamese people were lost, without eternal hope of any kind. Many American soldiers were dying without Christ. War was raging. God needed a person who had been broken, so He could use that person to declare His message of peace in the midst of a terrible conflict.

The Main Issue

Only one thing can keep you from experiencing the rule and reign of Christ in your life. That is a self-controlled life. This is the main issue. Can you trust God enough to surrender yourself completely to Christ?

Are you afraid to do this? Fear will paralyze you into taking no action. You can miss all that God wants to do in and through you because you are afraid to let go. You are afraid to turn loose and cast yourself completely into Christ's hands Fear whispers, "What will happen if you lose control?"

Above all else, we all need to be delivered from self. We need to be delivered from our own self-confidence.

All the issues we have discussed—secret sin, moral purity, discouragement, anger, bitterness, and many others, boil down to one issue, self-control. Our problems spring from our desire for the self-life—self-comfort, self-gratification, self-effort. We want to please ourselves, while Christ wants to take possession of us.

Paul was at the end of himself when he wrote, "For to me, to live is Christ and to die is gain" (Phil. 1:21).

Peter is a perfect example of a man who was totally broken. When Jesus said, "Follow me, and I will make you fishers of men," Peter immediately obeyed. Later, he would say, "We have left everything and followed You" (Matt. 19:27).

Peter was serious about his commitment to follow Jesus. He was loyal, faithful, and obedient.

When Jesus appeared before His disciples as he walked on the water in the midst of a storm, Peter said "Lord, if it is You, command me to come to You on the water" (Matt. 14:28).

When Jesus said, "Come," Peter immediately stepped out of the boat into the water.

He was a man who had unusual spiritual insight into the mysteries of God.

Jesus asked His disciples, "Who do you say that I am?"

Peter answered, "Thou art the Christ, the Son of the living God" (Matt. 16:16).

Jesus responded by saying, "Blessed are you, Simon Barjona, because flesh and blood did not reveal this to you, but My Father who is in heaven" (v. 17).

Immediately after this conversation, Jesus began to share that He was going to Jerusalem to suffer and die but that He would also rise from the dead on the third day.

Peter could not deal with this. He lost his gift of spiritual insight and wrapped himself in himself. He took Jesus aside and rebuked Him.

He had just declared that Jesus was the Son of the living God. Now he was rebuking his Lord. Can you imagine this?

Concerning what Jesus had said about His destiny in Jerusalem, Peter protested, "God forbid it, Lord! This shall never happen to You" (Matt. 16:22).

Moments after having blessed Peter for his spiritual insight, Jesus harshly rebuked him by saying, "Get behind Me, Satan! You are a stumbling block to Me; for you are not setting your mind on God's interests, but man's" (v. 23).

Here we see Peter being self-controlled. He was trusting his own wisdom and not the wisdom of God.

God says, "For My thoughts are not your thoughts, Neither are your ways My ways" (Isa. 55:8).

Peter forgot Jesus' requirement for discipleship: "If anyone wishes to come after Me, he must deny himself, and take up his cross and follow Me" (Matt. 16:24).

Peter's problem is too often our problem—a self-controlled life.

Jesus warned Peter that he would deny Him three times. He said, "Truly I say to you, that you yourself this very night, before a cock crows twice, shall three times deny Me" (Mark 14:30).

Still full of self-confidence Peter insisted, "Even if I have to die with You, I will not deny You!" (Mark 14:31).

Notice the dominance of what "I" will do.

Peter thought, "Maybe, Judas, maybe John, maybe James, but not me."

On the night before Jesus was crucified, Peter was outside the place where his Master was on trial. He was warming his hands by a fire when someone recognized him as a disciple of Christ. When he was asked if he knew Jesus, he denied it. Then someone insisted that he was a disciple because they could tell by his accent. Peter again declared that he was not a friend of Jesus. When the accusation was made a third time, he said, "Man, I do not know what you are talking about" (Luke 22:60).

That same verse says, "Immediately, while he was still speaking, a cock crowed."

This hit Peter like a ton of bricks, as if a roof fell in on him. He had denied his Lord three times. He was broken. He was through with self. Everything was surrendered to Christ. Now, God could begin to use him.

While we are obsessed with the individual sins that we think are hindering our spiritual walk, it is really the self-controlled-life that keeps God from using us.

Have you joined Paul at the altar of surrender and left, knowing that you are nothing and He is everything?

This is what Paul talks about when he wrote in Galatians 2:20, "I have been crucified with Christ; and it is no longer I who live, but Christ who lives in me; and the life which I now live in the flesh I live by faith in the Son of God, who loved me and gave Himself up for me."

Brokenness is a part of the progressive work of God in our lives. When you are broken, emptied, and completely at God's disposal, you will begin to know and experience His power. This is the beginning of experiencing the victorious and productive Christian life.

FOURTEEN

The End of the Story

What can God accomplish through one life which has been broken in order to be used by Him?

At the beginning of the 20th Century, spiritual coldness existed in the churches of Wales.

One day, a young man, Evan Roberts, was told, "You can miss any church meeting you want, but do not miss prayer meeting. If you do, you could miss a visitation of the Holy Spirit."

Roberts took heed and attended the prayer meetings. One night he heard a visiting evangelist preach on the subject, "Bend Me and Save My Nation."

God spoke to young Roberts that night. He prayed, "Bend me, Lord, break me and save my nation."

God heard his prayer and broke him until he became nothing and God became everything.

Evan Roberts went to churches throughout Wales. He shared the message God had given to him. The message had four points:

1. Confess all known sin
2. Turn from every sinful habit
3. Confess Christ as Lord publicly
4. Obey the Holy Spirit

He preached this message in every part of his nation. God sent a mighty spiritual awakening. How did this happen? It started with one man who prayed, "Bend Me, O Lord, bend me."

Evan Roberts arrived at the place where he realized that he could not live the Christian life in his own strength. He knew that he had to depend on the Holy Spirit, who was imparted to him at the time of his new birth in Christ.

Paul was at this same place when he cried, "Wretched man that I am!"

When the apostle had finally arrived at the end of himself, he discovered the secret of victory in the Christian life. Then he was able to write in Romans 7:25, "Thanks be to God through Jesus Christ our Lord!"

Are you at the end of yourself? Are you willing to pray, "Bend me, oh God?"

Can you pray, "Break me, oh God, break me?"

Within your heart, the untamed lion of "self" is roaring. Through brokenness, self can be dethroned and the power of God released to accomplish His will.

"Bend Me"

Evan Roberts experienced what Jesus said, "I am the vine, you are the branches; he who abides in Me and I in him, he bears much fruit, for apart from Me you can do nothing" (John 15:5).

Good oranges spring from good orange trees. Good grapes spring from good grape vines. You can always explain fruit's quality by going to its source.

In the production of grapes, the vine does the work. Its roots go deep into the ground, extending in search of good nourishment. They drink the moisture, absorb fertilizer, and generate the special sap which results in fruit.[1]

You may ask, "What about the branch? What does it do?"

A branch has only one concern—maintaining its relationship with the vine. If this relationship is right, life will flow into the branch. It will bear fruit. The branch simply lives in dependence on the vine, receiving what is given.[2]

This is exactly what Jesus wants us to understand about our relationship with Him. In John 15:5, He reveals the secret of living a victorious Christian life. He said, "apart from Me you can do nothing."

Don't miss the significance of the word *nothing*. If you want to be fruitful and victorious, become nothing so He becomes everything.

Evan Roberts was used by God to bring spiritual awakening to Wales. You will remember that it happened after he arrived totally to the end of himself and prayed, "Bend Me, O Lord and Save My Nation."

As he shared under God's anointing, churches that had been cold and empty began to be filled with people every night. So many people trusted Christ that all crime in the nation stopped completely. The police had nothing to do, so they formed choirs and sang in the nightly revival services.

Wales was a mining country. The miners depended on mules to move the ore. They used profane language to motivate these animals.

During the great revival, so many of the miners were converted and their vocabulary was so changed that the mules no longer could understand their commands.

In six months, more than 100,000 people in Wales gave their hearts and lives to Christ. This happened because one man was willing to become nothing so Christ could be everything.

Andrew Murray said, "The person who has something is not yet absolutely dependent. The person who has nothing is absolutely dependent."[3]

You may work diligently for God, expending much energy, and still not have the manifestation of His power in your life and ministry. Why? This will happen if you try to do the work of the Vine instead of accepting your role as a branch.

What is "branch work"? It is becoming totally dependent on the vine to do all the work.

In John 4:46-53, you can read the story of a royal official whose son lay sick in the city of Capernaum. The boy was near to death. When the father heard that Jesus was visiting his area, he went to meet Him. He begged our Lord to go to his home and heal his son.

Jesus simply said, "Go your way; your son lives" (v. 50).

That was it. The royal official turned and started his journey back to Capernaum. All he had was the word of Jesus—nothing more. He rested with complete confidence in Christ.

Now, read what happened: "As he was now going down, his slaves met him, saying that his son was living. So he inquired of them the hour when he began to get better. Then they said to him, 'Yesterday at the seventh hour the fever left him.'

"So the father knew that it was at that hour in which Jesus said to him, 'Your son lives;' and he himself believed, and his whole household" (vv. 51-53).

This is a story of complete dependence on God and of real faith. The father was at the end of himself. He trusted Jesus completely and allowed Him to become everything.

What does being totally surrendered to Christ mean?

It means that you give up all rights to yourself. You bring all of your riches, talents, pride, abilities and lack of abilities, your mind, heart, body, and soul to Christ. You yield everything to Him.

This demands that you know the answer to another question. How do you do this?

You must arrive at the end of yourself. You must become nothing, so He can become everything.

True belief and total surrender occur when you trust God to do what He says. You yield yourself to Him. You believe and obey—whatever the circumstance or cost might be.

In Galatians 2:20, Paul summed it all up when he wrote, "I have been crucified with Christ; and it is no longer I who live, but Christ lives in me; and the life which I now live in the flesh I live by faith in the Son of God, who loved me and gave Himself up for me."

The Stockdale Paradox

What is faith? The Bible defines it as "the assurance (the confirmation, the title-deed) of the things [we] hope for, being the proof of things [we] do not see and the conviction of their reality—faith perceiving as real fact what is not revealed to the senses" (Heb. 11:1, *The Amplified Bible*).

Notice that the essence of true faith is not some quality in ourselves. The strength of our faith is not what saves us or what keeps us saved; it is the object of our faith—Jesus Christ. Faith is trusting in Jesus to save us from sin. It is being certain that He is who He is. It is knowing that He can and will do what He says He will do.

After you are saved by faith, continue to live by faith. This is the place in which you may encounter a problem. As a child, I was saved by faith, but Satan wanted to hinder my living by faith.

To live by faith, you must not have a false hope. Your dependence must be only in the object of your hope—Jesus.

In his book, *Good to Great*, Jim Collins relates his encounter with Admiral Jim Stockdale, the highest-ranking United States military officer held in the "Hanoi Hilton" prisoner-of-war prison during the Vietnam War.[4] Admiral Stockdale was imprisoned for eight years—1965 to 1973. He suffered torture more than 20 times. Throughout his ordeal, he had no prisoner's rights. He was never certain whether he would ever see his family again. He took command and did everything possible to create conditions that would allow other prisoners to survive unbroken. Constantly, he fought an internal war against his captors. He refused to be used for propaganda purposes. He even beat himself with a stool and cut himself with a razor to deliberately disfigure himself, so he could not be shown on videotape as an example of a "well-treated" prisoner.

Through their letters he exchanged with his wife secret intelligence information, knowing that if he were discovered, it would mean more torture and possible death. He instituted rules that would help people to deal with torture. He also invented an elaborate internal communications system to reduce the sense of isolation that his captors sought to create. Under his leadership, the prisoners used a matrix of tap codes for the alpha characters.

How did he do all of this and survive? He said, "I never lost faith in the end of the story. I never doubted, not only that I would get out but also that I would prevail in the end and turn the experience into the defining event of my life, which in retrospect, I would not trade."

Collins asked him, "Who did not make it out?"

"Oh, that is easy," he said, "The optimists."

Surprised, Collins asked, "The optimists?"

"Oh," replied Stockdale, "they were the ones who said, 'We're going to be out by Christmas.' And Christmas would come, and Christmas would go. Then they would say, 'We're going to be out by Easter.' And Easter would come and go. And then by Thanksgiving, and then it would be Christmas again. And they died of broken hearts."

He then said to Collins, "This is a very important lesson. You must never confuse faith that you will prevail in the end—which you can never afford to lose—with the discipline to confront the most brutal facts of your current reality, whatever they might be."

He told the optimists, "We're not getting out by Christmas. Deal with it."

Here is the Stockdale paradox: "Retain faith that you will prevail in the end, regardless of difficulties, and at the same time confront the most brutal facts of your current reality, whatever they may be."

We can confront the realities of our issues, such as anger, guilt, bitterness, and discouragement. However, the object of our faith is Jesus. He has already overcome all of these things on our behalf. We know the "end of the story"!

[1]Andrew Murray, *Absolute Surrender* (Vereeniging, South Africa: Christian Art Publishers, 1930), 133.

[2] Ibid., 132.

[3]Murray, 135.

[4]Jim Collins, *Good to Great* (New York: HarperCollins, 2001), 83-86.

PART IV

SECRET OF LORDSHIP

FIFTEEN

The Ring

As I think about the relationship I have with God, the Father, I'm reminded of the preciousness of a wedding ring. A ring represents a deep and abiding love between two people. It is circular, indicating that this love is to be without an end in this world.

My first wife, Sherry, had given me such a ring. It symbolized our love for one another. It reminded us of our vows to be faithful to each other until we were parted by death.

Sherry had my name, along with the date of our wedding, engraved on the inside of the band. It was special. I wore it with pride. I was proud of her and proud to be her husband.

On December 4, 1993, Sherry died suddenly in our home in Belo Horizonte. That was the day that Sherry went to heaven. But something else happened. That day, she ceased being my wife. I could never have prepared myself to deal with this reality. It was the most difficult day of my life.

Four weeks later, I attended the New Year's Eve service at our church—Barro Preto Baptist Church in Belo Horizonte. This was something Sherry and I had done together since arriving in Brazil. It had become a meaningful time when we joined our hands and hearts, reflected on our lives over the past year, and committed ourselves to what was ahead.

That night, I didn't want to look back on what had just happened. I wasn't at all sure what was ahead for me. I knew that I had to find a way to get through the deep pain and grief

I was experiencing. I had to find a way to survive, but I didn't know what path it would take me down or how long that path would be.

During the final hour before midnight, I was praying alone and reflecting. Then, I saw it—the ring. As I studied it and all that it symbolized, I realized that Sherry no longer was my wife. What should I do with this ring? Should I continue to wear it, letting it say that I was still married to her?

In that moment, I decided to confront my grief with all the reality that I could marshal. Tearfully, I began slowly working the ring off of my finger.

Oh, the pain of that act!

It was tough. I was pulling away a part of my body, but it sealed my determination to do everything necessary to move forward. As the ring finally slipped from my finger, I said, "Sherry, I love you; but you are no longer my wife."

Christ teaches that no marriages exist in Heaven. We are the bride; He is the Groom. Wonderfully, we are wedded to Him in a relationship that is eternal.

The Bible teaches that when we accepted Christ as Lord and Savior, "by one Spirit we were all baptized into one body" (1 Cor. 12:13).

Christ enters our lives by means of the Holy Spirit. His presence is God's seal on us, marking us for redemption. His indwelling assures us that we are the children of God.

In Ephesians 1:13-14, Paul was inspired to write, "Having also believed, you were sealed in Him with the Holy Spirit of promise, who is given as a pledge of our inheritance, with a view to the redemption of God's own possession."

You can be confident that the Holy Spirit will not withdraw Himself from you when you commit a sin. You are secure in Him. This is true because Christ has bought you with His own blood.

In Ephesians 1:7, Paul wrote, "In Him we have redemption through His blood, the forgiveness of our trespasses, according to the riches of His grace."

As a Christian, you are marked with God's seal—the Holy Spirit. He is a deposit, guaranteeing our inheritance as our Father's children and as the bride of Christ. Once these relationships are established, they never can be broken.

Many years ago, my earthly father shared a powerfully encouraging verse with me, Romans 8:38: "For I am convinced that neither death, nor life, nor angels, nor principalities, nor things present, nor things to come, nor powers, nor height, nor depth, nor any other created thing, shall be able to separate us from the love of God, which is in Christ Jesus our Lord."

Having the presence of the Holy Spirit in your life is evidence of your lasting relationship with the Father and His Son, Jesus. This is called eternal life.

In marriage, the ring symbolizes both love and a unique commitment. But, unlike eternal life, it will not last forever. On the other hand, the Holy Spirit is our eternal Ring. He is our guarantee that the love of Christ in us will endure. Not even death can separate us from that relationship.

The Holy Spirit is the third person of the Trinity. He enters into your life the moment you surrender your life to Christ as Lord. One of the most empowering results of this surrender is the filling of the Holy Spirit. This means to be controlled by Him.

In spite of this great empowering privilege, as a believer, you can still sin against the Holy Spirit. This happens when your old self-nature retakes the control of your life.

You can sin against the Holy Spirit in two ways: grieving Him and quenching Him.

Grieving the Spirit

Paul warned us, "Do not grieve the Holy spirit of God, by whom you were sealed for the day of redemption" (Eph. 4:30). He restates that, as believers, we are "sealed unto the day of redemption." This means that grieving the Holy Spirit is not a sin that can cause you to lose your salvation.

Billy Graham says that *grieve* is a love word.[1] When you lose to death someone you love, it hurts. You experience much pain in the soul. You can only suffer grief over people, but you can cause this hurt and pain to the Holy Spirit when you grieve Him.

What happens when you grieve the Holy Spirit?

Billy Graham recalls walking through a textile factory near his home in North Carolina. Hundreds of looms were spinning cloth. Each of them made fine linen threads. The mill manager explained that the machinery was so delicate that if even one of the entire 30,000 threads broke, all the looms would instantly stop. To illustrate, he broke a thread. When the break had been repaired, all of the machines started again.[2]

This is a good illustration of what happens when a believer sins. Your life is impaired. It has a broken thread. The Holy Spirit is grieved because He loves you. Until your sin problem is repaired, your Christian life will lose its joy and peace. You will be without power to serve and love.

Quenching the Spirit

Paul also admonishes us, "Do not quench (suppress or subdue) the [Holy] Spirit" (1 Thess. 5:19, *The Amplified Bible*.)

In other words, "Do not put out the Spirit's fire."

Quenching the Holy Spirit does not mean that you expel Him from your life. It does mean that you have extinguished the love and power that He wants to manifest in and through you.

You can put out a fire by throwing water on it or by smothering it with dirt. The Holy Spirit is seeking to work in and through your life, but you can choose to ignore Him. By doing this, you can put out the fire of the Spirit.

You are quenching the Holy Spirit when you refuse to obey His voice, guidance, and leadership.

The Hickory Stick

What will happen to you if, after you become a Christian, you choose to sin? If you persist in grieving and quenching the Holy Spirit, God will deal with you in one of two ways.

First is the old-fashioned "hickory stick." In other words, God will give you a good spanking.

All of my three children are now adults, but I still remember how I reacted when they were children and disobeyed. What did I do? Did I kick them out of our house and tell them never to return? No. I am their father. I love them deeply. I chose to discipline them. All three of them got spankings. Why? Because, I really do love them.

Your heavenly Father loves you. He says, "My son, do not regard lightly the discipline of the lord, nor faint when you are reproved by him; for those whom the Lord loves He disciplines, and He scourges every son whom He receives" (Heb. 12:5-6).

If you are really a child of God and you deliberately fall into sin, God, your Father, will discipline you in a strong manner.

Someone may say glibly, "Well, I gave my heart to Christ. Now I can sin all I want to. Nothing will happen."

That person had better beware. The Bible says, "Now if you are exempt from correction and left without discipline in which all [of God's children] share, then you are illegitimate offspring and not true sons [at all]" (Heb. 12:8, *The Amplified Bible*).

If a person says that he is a Christian, but he continues in sin, never knowing the discipline of the Father, he is fooling himself. He is not a child of God. God is not his Father. Jesus is not his Lord. The Holy Spirit does not dwell in him. He is not in the family of God.

All Christians do sin, but we do not have to. We can live one full day without grieving or quenching the Holy Spirit. If we can live without sin one day, we can also live without sin for two days, *et cetera*.

Do you see the potential of your life in Christ? Why settle for less?

When Satan tempts you, you make a deliberate choice whether or not to sin. If you yield to the temptation, you are at fault. You—not the devil—are the one who is responsible. You have reverted to living a self-controlled life.

The Filling of the Holy Spirit

To be filled by the Holy Spirit means to be dominated and controlled by Him. Being Spirit filled is the key to living a victorious Christian life.

In Ephesians 5:18, Paul cautioned, "Do not get drunk with wine, for that is debauchery; but be filled and stimulated with the (Holy) Spirit," (Eph. 5:18, *The Amplified Bible*).

Notice several important things about the verb "be filled" in this critical verse.

First, it is a command. This verb is in the imperative mood. It is like telling your child to shut the door. You are giving a command. There are no options.

Secondly, it is in the passive voice in the Greek language. It means that you cannot do this yourself. It is an action that has to be done to you. This is important. The Holy Spirit does the filling and controlling.

Thirdly, it is a continuous action. It is not a one-time act. Billy Graham says, "We are not filled once and for all like a bucket."[3]

Merrill C. Tenney has compared this to the situation in some old-time farmhouse kitchens. A sink was in one corner. Above the sink was a pipe that carried a continuous stream of water from a spring on the outside. This constant supply kept the sink full of good water. In the same way, as a believer, you are to be constantly filled with the Holy Spirit. His supply is endless, never ceasing, until you stop it by sin. You should never be emptied of His joy and power.[4]

Jesus said, "He who believes in Me, as the Scripture said, 'From his innermost being shall flow rivers of living water.' But this He spoke of the Spirit" (John 7:38-39).

Rejoice! The supply of Living Water is never exhausted.

Often, you will hear someone speak of having an experience which they will refer to as a "second baptism", "second blessing", or "second work of grace." None of these experiences can be found in the Bible. The Bible speaks of only one baptism of the Holy Spirit.

In 1 Corinthians 12:13, Paul wrote, "For by one Spirit we were all baptized into one body, whether Jews or Greeks, whether slaves or free, and we were all made to drink of one Spirit."

When you surrender to Christ as Lord, you receive all the Holy Spirit you will ever have or need. You do not receive the Holy Spirit in parts. You receive a full measure of Him.[5]

As a believer, your concern should not be whether you have the Holy Spirit, but whether He has you under His control.

Experience a constant filling of the Holy Spirit. Just as a stream of life-giving water will, if unhindered by any blockage, continually flow from a limitless source, He wants to be always filling and controlling you.

Remember: when you grieve or quench Him, you can create a dam that will hinder the filling of the Spirit. When this happens, you have stepped back from being Spirit-controlled. You are self-controlled. The flow of His power and joy has been blocked.

Being filled with the Holy Spirit enables you to glorify Christ. Concerning the work of the Holy Spirit, Jesus taught, "He shall glorify Me, for He shall take of Mine and shall disclose it to you" (John 16:14).

In 1 Corinthians 10:31, Paul wrote, "Whether, then, you eat or drink or whatever you do, do all to the glory of God."

Stop and think about what you just read. You are to do everything in such a way that God will be glorified.

Living a holy life in your own strength is impossible; but being filled with the Holy Spirit makes the impossible possible. His filling gives you power for ministry. He enables you to witness effectively for Christ. As a Spirit-filled person, you can live a godly life, constantly experiencing His peace and joy.

How to Be Filled With the Holy Spirit

Often, concerned Christians ask me how to be filled with the Holy Spirit. I am quick to tell them that the Bible does not give us a formula. Then, I stress that two things are essential if you would know His filling. First, you must confess and repent of every sin.

Miss Bertha Smith was a godly missionary who served for many years in China. I was always blessed and stirred when I heard her speak. When she spoke on the "Holiness of God" and the "Holy Spirit," she told everyone in her audience to go home, get on their knees before God, and ask Him to reveal every sin in their life, from their past to the present day. Then, she would instruct them to write down a sin list.

If you do this, God likely will remind you of unkind treatment toward someone, even in years past; bitterness; jealousy; pride; unclean thoughts; laziness; gluttony, etc.

Next, answer the question, "Who is really ruling my life?"

Submission is the second requirement for being filled with the Holy Spirit. Only when Christ is on the throne of your life can you experience the Spirit's power and blessing. Jesus demands your full commitment to Him as Lord. He said, "If anyone wishes to come after Me, let him deny himself, and take up his cross daily, and follow Me" (Luke 9:23).

Billy Graham defines *submission* as renouncing our own way and seeking above all else to submit to Christ as Lord and being ruled by Him in every area of our lives.[6]

In other words, you can know that you are a Spirit-filled person when you have rejected self-control and placed Christ at the center of your life. Allow Him to reign as your Lord.

This is an act of your will. You can make a choice to yield your life into Christ's hands.

In his letter to the Romans, Paul admonished believers, "Therefore do not let sin reign in your mortal body so that you should obey its lusts, and do not go on presenting the members of your body to sin as instruments of unrighteousness; but present yourselves to God as those alive from the dead, and your members as instruments of righteousness to God" (Rom. 6:12-13).

The word *offer* means to yield. Billy Graham says that it means to place yourself at the disposal of someone.[7]

Submission, which removes any hindrance to the Holy Spirit's filling, is the absolute, unconditional surrender of your life to Christ. It is your saying to Him, without any reservations, "Be my Lord."

Decide this question: Will you rule and control your life, or will you choose to allow the Holy Spirit to control you?

A man and a woman can have a marriage license and can be legally husband and wife but not be totally committed to each other. When they stand at the altar and exchange vows, they must be absolutely sincere. The reason that it was so painful for me to take Sherry's ring from my finger was that it symbolized a deep heart commitment that I had made to her.

You can say that Jesus is your Lord, but can you say this sincerely? Is He really in control of your life? Have you made a heart commitment to Him? Have you decided to be completely His?

When you are totally surrendered to Christ, you do not have to fret; the Holy Spirit will fill you. You will have His power and leadership.

Surrendering to Christ is something that you do moment by moment and day by day. Even though being a Christian means that you have the permanent indwelling of the Holy Spirit, you cannot claim one filling and then expect to live victoriously under your own control. Daily, exercise your will and decide to allow Him to control you. When you do this, you will experience the full measure of His grace.

The Holy Spirit is the first secret of living under the lordship of Christ 24 hours a day, seven days a week. As you are daily filled (controlled) by the Holy Spirit, you will experience His power.

[1]Billy Graham, *The Holy Spirit* (Nashville: W Publishing Group, 1978), 160.
[2]Ibid., 160.
[3]Ibid., 117.
[4]Ibid.
[5]John 3:34.
[6]Graham, 140.
[7]Graham, 143.

SIXTEEN

How to Stop a Truck

Often, during my church-planting trainings, I ask my audiences, "How many of you would stand in the middle of a highway, lift your hands, and try to stop a big, 18-wheeler truck that is coming straight toward you? Does anyone have the courage to do that?"

Of course, no one does.

Then, I share that this is exactly what I saw one very tiny woman do in Zambia. Everyone is stunned. I can see it on their faces. They know that I am a missionary and am not supposed to tell lies, but they think I'm describing something that is impossible.

Smiling, I explain, "Yes, one small woman stepped out onto the highway, raised her hands, and stopped a huge truck that was coming straight toward her. How did she do it? She was a Zambian police officer."

She had the full authority of the Zambian government behind her.

This is what having power means.

The word that is translated *power* in the New Testament is the equivalent of our modern word "dynamite." In other words, God is all-powerful. His power is explosive.

Isaiah, the Old Testament prophet, saw God on His throne.[1] A throne is a place of power and authority.

In the third chapter of Acts, we find an interesting story that illustrates the great truth about the little African woman's ability to stop a truck. Peter and John were going up to the temple for afternoon prayers. Their habit was to have a time of prayer in the morning and again at 3 in the afternoon. This was also a time of sacrifice. Because of this, many people visited the temple in the afternoon.

As they were about to enter the temple, they encountered a crippled man. Since his birth, he had not been able to walk. Every day, someone carried him to his spot just outside the temple gate that was called Beautiful. He was there to beg for money.

Can you imagine how low his self-esteem must have been? He was not strong enough to work and be a productive member of society. Every day, his life was reduced to begging.

Yet, this was a good place for him, because the rabbis taught that there were three pillars for the Jewish faith: the Torah, worship, and the showing of kindness.

Giving alms was one of the main ways to show kindness. It was considered a major way of expressing one's love for God. For these reasons, sitting at the gate called Beautiful at the time of worship and sacrifice was a good place and a good time for him.

As Peter and John approached, the crippled man reached out his hand and begged, "Alms . . . Alms . . . Alms."

Normally, people would put a coin in his hand, or they would completely ignore him. This is what he expected. On this day, something totally unexpected happened.

Peter and John stopped and looked at him as though he was a person of great value. Then, Peter said, "Look at us!"

Startled, the beggar looked up, giving Peter his full attention.

What Peter said next surprised the man even more. He said, "I do not possess silver and gold, but what I do have I give to you: In the name of Jesus Christ the Nazarene — walk!"[2]

John Polhill says, "The reference to 'the name' is not incidental."[3]

In the biblical sense, a name is far more than a label by which to call someone. A name represented the extension of one's personality and being. To invoke the name of Jesus is to call upon His authority and power.

Peter took the crippled man by the right hand and helped him to stand up. Instantly the man's feet and ankles became strong. He jumped to his feet and began to walk. I can see him grabbing Peter and shouting, "I can walk! I can walk! I can walk!"

And walk he did. He not only walked; he began to run and jump and praise God at the top of his voice. He was so excited that he ran inside the temple, leaping and shouting praises to God.

This was indeed a miracle. Because of Levitical law, all his life this man had been denied access to the inside of the temple. He was considered blemished. The law said, "No man of your offspring throughout their generations who has a defect shall approach to offer the food of his God. For no one who has a defect shall approach: a blind man, or a lame man, or he who has a disfigured face, or any deformed limb, or a man who has a broken foot or broken hand, or a hunchback or a dwarf, or one who has a defect in his eye or eczema or scabs or crushed testicles. No man among the descendants of Aaron the priest, who has a defect, is to come near to offer the Lord's offerings by fire; since he has a defect, he shall not come near to offer the bread of his God" (Lev. 21:17-21).

Can you imagine this scene? All of his life he had sat on the outside. Now he was on the inside. He was not only on the inside of the temple; he was healed physically and spiritually. He was fully accepted by the Lord. He was inside the temple. Christ was inside his life. In one miraculous moment, he went from being an outsider to being an insider.

How did this happen? It was not because of any power and authority that Peter and John possessed in and of themselves. It happened the same way the little African woman stopped the big truck. These apostles acted under the authority of someone else. They acted in the name of someone with absolute power—someone who is superior. They acted in the name of Jesus.

Both of these stories, the one about a little woman standing in the middle of an African highway and the one about two sensitive men confronting a crippled beggar, illustrate a great truth about how we are to live our lives. We are to live under the authority of Jesus Christ. He said, "All authority has been given to Me in heaven and on earth" (Matt. 28:18).

When we live under His authority and act in His name, we will see God glorifying Himself by working miracles in and through us.

Phoch Hai

Vietnamese may not be the toughest language to learn but, because it is tonal, it is extremely difficult for an American. The language has five different tones. If you say the word *ma* and make the word go straight up with a high tone it means one thing. If you lower the tone, it means something else. You can say it in a flat monotone and give it another meaning. Again, you can change the meaning by modulating the tone. The meaning of every word is determined by its tonal treatment.

Being a person of high expectations, I arrived in Vietnam determined to preach my first sermon in Vietnamese, without using any notes, within a year. I wrote out a lengthy message that fully explained the gospel. I named each of the Ten Commandments and discussed how we have broken all of them. My sermon went into great detail about Jesus' death to be our sin solution, and about His resurrection. I was careful to deal with exactly how a person can receive Christ personally into his life. I decided that while I might not be able to ask for a wrench or hammer, I would be able to tell people how to be saved.

After nine, mind-numbing and grueling months of study, I was finally ready to preach in Vietnamese, using only my Bible. With great enthusiasm, I went to a little mission called Phouch Hai in the South Vietnamese city of Nha Trang City. When I arrived, the small building was packed with people. It was located just behind a United States Air Force base. Fighter jets and cargo planes constantly took off and landed. The building had no nursery, so everywhere I looked, mothers held crying babies. The situation was chaotic. What a setting for preaching my one sermon over which I had labored for almost a year!

When I stood, just remembering each word and its proper tone was an exhausting struggle. At the end of message, I was drained mentally and emotionally, but I was also happy. I said, "If anyone would like to give their life to Christ, please just stand up where you are."

When no one stood, I believed that I had totally failed to clarify the gospel. With all the noise and confusion, I had missed many words and tones. Devastated, I bowed my head and prayed, "Lord, forgive me for being such a failure."

When I looked up, a woman stood. Addressing the congregation, she said, "I want to give my life to Jesus."

This woman demonstrated awesome courage in order to do this. She was from animist and Buddhist backgrounds. The Holy Spirit had used the message I had struggled to deliver to touch her heart, convict her of sin, and draw her to Christ.

On the way back to my little apartment, God showed me a powerful truth: When we are at the end of ourselves and allow Him to control us, He will do His work in and through us.

He caused me to remember what the Bible says in Zechariah 4:6, "'Not by might nor by power, but by My Spirit,' says the Lord of hosts."

God was saying, "Wade, you will not produce fruit by your abilities, talents, and eloquent speaking. You will produce fruit by My power, as My Spirit works in and through you."

Power is authority. It is the ability to influence. In order to see supernatural results in your life and ministry, the power of God must be released through you. Living under the authority of the Holy Spirit is the second secret of living under the lordship of Christ.

[1]Isaiah 6:1.

[2]Acts 3:6.

[3]John Polhill, *The New American Commentary: Acts* (Nashville: Broadman Press, 1992), 128.

SEVENTEEN

Listen. God Is Saying Something

Everyone is born with a huge hole in his or her inner being. That person's spirit is empty. Everywhere I go, I find people desperately trying to fill that emptiness.

In the New Testament Book of John, you can read the story of a very moral and religious man—Nicodemus. He was a respected Jewish leader and an important member of a religious party called the Pharisees.

Outwardly, Nicodemus seemed to have his life in order; but, on the inside, something was missing. Knowing this, he arrived, under the cover of darkness, seeking time alone with Jesus.

Immediately, he was confronted with one of the most startling and crucial statements Jesus ever made. He was told, "Unless one is born again, he cannot see the kingdom of God" (John 3:3).

Nicodemus was baffled. He thought that Jesus was being absurd, telling him that he had to go through the process of physical birth a second time.

Jesus explained that He was talking about the necessity of a spiritual birth. He said, "Unless one is born of water and the Spirit, he cannot enter into the kingdom of God" (John 3:5).

Birth by water is possibly a reference to the physical birth of a baby. Jesus said clearly that being born of the Spirit is spiritual. This is what happens when someone commits his or her life to Christ as Lord and Savior. At that moment, the Holy Spirit begins living in that person.

How do you define eternal life? Jesus said, "This is eternal life, that they may know Thee, the only true God, and Jesus Christ whom Thou hast sent" (John 17:3).

This is fundamental. Apart from being born again, a person cannot know God nor have the assurance that that person is His child.

What Does Knowing God Mean?

My wife, Barbara, and I were teaching during a Pioneer Evangelism conference in South Africa. In one of the sessions, I asked if anyone knew that country's president. A man raised his hand and said, "Yes."

After learning his name, I asked the man, "When was the last time that you had dinner with the president?"

Everyone laughed. I followed with, "What is the president's favorite music? What is his favorite color?"

Abashed, the man from my audience admitted that he did not know the president of South Africa personally. He had helped me to illustrate that a big difference exists in knowing about someone and really knowing someone.

In John 17:3, Jesus taught us that having eternal life means to know both God the Father and His Son, Jesus, personally. The result of knowing our Lord personally is to have forgiveness of sin and the assurance of eternity with Him in Heaven.

How can you grow in a deeper and more personal knowledge of God?

My Early-Morning Prayer Experience

Some years ago, I heard a preacher challenge everyone in his audience to know God on a deeper level. He talked about how the great English preacher, Charles Spurgeon, had been used to turn his nation upside down for Christ.

He asked, "Do you want God to be able to use you in this way?"

Since I surrendered control of my life to Him, I have been consumed with a deep hunger for God to use me mightily. I answered the preacher's question with a heartfelt, "Yes."

After a brief pause, allowing his question to soak in, the speaker told how it was Spurgeon's habit to get up at 4 every morning and to spend four hours in prayer.

"If that is the secret to God's power," I thought, "I will do that as well."

Determined, I asked a carpenter friend to build a special kneeling altar for my living room. I was ready to follow in Spurgeon's steps. But, the preacher had left out of his story one small fact. England's "Prince of Preachers" lived more than 100 years ago, during an era when no electricity existed. Like most other people of his time, he went to bed early. He easily could wake at 4 every morning.

Not thinking about this, I went to bed at my usual time— about midnight. When my alarm went off at 4, my body protested that it was not ready to rise and shine.

Somehow, I struggled out of bed, stumbled into the living room, fell onto my knees at my new altar, and, within five minutes, I was sound asleep. I awoke with the realization that I had made a commitment to pray for four hours. With renewed resolve, I began, "Lord, bless my wife up there in that bed."

As I spoke the words, I could see her sleeping so peaceful-ly, while I was suffering in the living room. Pushing that image from my mind and refocusing on prayer, I pleaded, "Bless my daughter, my sons, my dad, my mom, my brother, my sister, my uncle, and my aunt."

Sneaking a peek at my watch, I was stunned to realize that I had been praying for all of three minutes. I wondered, "How in the world am I ever going to spend four hours at this?"

That morning, in 1976, I realized that even though I had been born again and called to the ministry, had been the pastor of three churches, had served as a missionary in Vietnam, and was then engaged in evangelistic work in Washington, D. C., I did not really know God in a deep and profound way. Alone on my knees, I woke up spiritually. Earnestly, I prayed, "God, teach me to pray."

When I finally got up from my knees at that altar, I had learned that the secret to having power for life and ministry is not praying four hours every day. The secret is learning how to know God.

Hearing God

After that early-morning prayer experience, God showed me something that has changed my whole Christian life. He taught me the importance of learning how to listen when He speaks.

Jesus said, "He who has ears, let him hear" (Matt. 13:43).

Again, in Revelation 2:7, He said, "He who has an ear, let him hear what the Spirit says to the churches."

Hearing the Father and obeying Him were the reasons for Jesus' success in life and ministry. He said, "For I did not speak on My own initiative, but the Father Himself who sent Me has given Me commandment, what to say, and what to speak. And I know that His commandment is eternal life; therefore the things I speak, I speak just as the Father has told Me" (John 12:49-50).

One of the functions of the Holy Spirit is to guide us as believers.

Jesus said, "But I tell you the truth, it is to your advantage that I go away; for if I do not go away, the Helper shall not come to you; but if I go, I will send Him to you. But when He, the Spirit of truth, comes, He will guide you into all the truth; for He will not speak on His own initiative, but whatever He hears, He will speak; and He will disclose to you what is to come" (John 16:7,13).

When you learn to listen to God, the Holy Spirit will speak to you through your spiritual ears. He will tell you the truth about the crucial issues of your life. When you must pass through times of great darkness, He will light your way. He will be the Counselor you can trust.

In John 15:5, Jesus said, "I am the vine, you are the branches; he who abides in Me, and I in him, he bears much fruit, for apart from Me you can do nothing."

Producing fruit for God is impossible for us. God produces His fruit through us. This is why we must learn to abide in Christ. This means to live in vital union with Him.

Abiding in Christ is essential for four reasons:

1. We are to produce fruit (John 15:4).

2. We are to produce more fruit (v. 2).

3. We are to produce much fruit (v. 5).

4. We are to produce fruit that remains (v. 16).

To be a fruitful Christian, abide in Christ. How do you do this? Constantly listen to God.

You may ask, "How will God speak to me?"

He speaks primarily through His inspired word—the Holy Bible. This book is inerrant, which means it is without error. You can trust the Bible. Its Scriptures are God-breathed. They are God's personal love letter to you. When you read the Bible, God speaks just to you.

Why should you read the Bible? Read it for one reason only—to hear what God is saying to you. Listen: He is saying something important.

After that humiliating morning at my altar in 1976, I learned some practical things about how to listen to God as you read His Word. I'll share them with you.

First, understand that you are not committing to read the entire Bible in one year. Your sole purpose is to read so that you can hear God speaking to you. Select one of the Bible's books for your reading. While any of its 66 books will do, I suggest beginning in the New Testament with Paul's letter to the Ephesians. This wonderful little book will teach you who you are in Christ.

As you read, do three things. First, ask God to show you the spiritual truths in each verse. Always begin by praying, "Lord, show me the truths in each of the verses I will read today."

Ephesians 1:1 reads, "Paul, an apostle of Christ Jesus by the will of God, to the saints who are at Ephesus and who are faithful in Christ Jesus:"

Here is how the Holy Spirit spoke to my spiritual ears as I read that verse. He showed me three truths:

1. Paul was an apostle of Jesus Christ by the will of God.

2. The letter was written to the "saints" in Ephesus.

3. The letter was written to the "faithful in Christ Jesus."

Before I learned to listen to God, a verse such as this made no sense to me. I would just skip over it. Now, I stop, wait, and meditate. By my really listening, the Holy Spirit was able to show me these three truths.

Next, ask God to personalize each truth. Ask, "Lord, what are you saying just to me?"

To hear what He is saying, you must stop and listen. Do not rush through your Bible reading. Wait for God to speak.

As I read Ephesians 1:1 on the Brazilian mission field, here is how God personalized it for me:

First, He said, "Thomas Wade, you are a disciple of Jesus Christ by my will."

He reminded me that I am a Christian because of His grace, His mercy, His sovereignty, and His will. I was amazed when I realized the deep things He was revealing to me about who I am in Christ.

Then He said, "Thomas Wade, you are my saint in Brazil."

This really got my attention, because we do not normally see ourselves as saints. In reality, a saint is any person whom God has set apart for Himself. As believers, you and I are saints.

Finally, God said, "Thomas Wade, I want you to be faithful to Jesus Christ until the day you die."

As I waited and meditated, I could hear an inner voice impressing my mind with these thoughts. I knew the Holy Spirit was speaking to me through this verse.

When you have allowed God to speak to you from a verse and personalize it for you, pray back to Him the truths He has taught you. Learn to praise and thank God.

When God spoke to me so powerfully from Ephesians 1, I prayed, "Thank you Lord, that You called me by Your will. Thank You that You called me to be Your saint in Brazil."

Then, in light of the third truth He had taught me, I prayed, "Lord, by Your grace, keep me faithful to Christ until death."

By allowing God to reveal and personalize truths from the Scripture, then praying these back to Him, I know that I am always praying in the will of God, because I am praying the Word of God.

When God has finished speaking to you from one verse, go on to the next. Keep praying through each verse in Ephesians. Then, select another book of the Bible.

If you do this day after day, week after week, month after month, year after year, verse after verse, book after book, you will get to know God in a deep and personal way. This has been my discovery. When the Holy Spirit gives me a truth, I underline or mark it. Since 1976, my Bibles are filled with personal notes regarding what God has been teaching me.

As you learn to listen, God will speak directly to your heart at times. The Holy Spirit may strongly impress your mind.

You can understand how to know if it is the Holy Spirit or Satan speaking to you. I know of a simple test. The Holy Spirit will never tell you to do something that is contrary to God's Word.

A woman once told me, "The Holy Spirit told me to divorce my husband and marry another man."

She was confused and wrong. The Holy Spirit did not tell her that. He always leads a person into truth. He teaches the principles clearly laid out in the Bible. He never contradicts the Word of God.

The Shirt

Here is an illustration of how God can speak by impressing your heart and mind:

While serving as a missionary in Brazil, I often needed to travel to cities in the interior of our state of Minas Gerais. For one or two days, I would drive around in my truck, using loudspeakers to advertise an evangelistic meeting that I would conduct in the city plaza. Large crowds always gathered on the evening of this event after hearing the many advertisements promising to show the most inspiring true film ever made—The Life and Death of Jesus Christ, produced by Campus Crusade for Christ.

One night, over a thousand people were standing in an open field in the small city of Corinto. By Brazilian standards, it was cold.

At the end of film, I shared a brief message on the cross of Christ. I shared this message using fluorescent paints and a black light. I finished by drawing a big red cross in the center of the board. When the black light was turned on, the crowd stood silent and still. Everyone was staring, because now the paint depicting the cross glowed brightly.

Quickly, I did what I have done hundreds of times before thousands of people. I invited the viewers to give their lives to Christ. I asked those who were willing to do this to walk forward and stand in front of my truck. I promised to pray with them and to give them some helpful literature.

I recall that on this night, many people responded. I prayed with them as a group and asked the fellow believers from the area to help distribute the literature. After this, how-

ever, I asked anyone who had a special need to stand in a line
so that I could pray for them. As had been my custom, I met
with the people who were willing to wait in the line one by
one. I listened to personal problems, needs, and descriptions
of sickness.

Before I prayed for each person, I asked about his or her
spiritual condition. I had discovered that these prayer lines
opened the door for leading many people to Christ.

That night in Corinto, something special happened. At the
very end of the prayer line was a young man. He said, "I use
drugs. I am poor. I am so poor that I do not even have a shirt
on my back."

When I looked up, I was startled to see that he was indeed
standing in the cold without a shirt.

God said to me, "Wade, give him your shirt."

"No!" I silently protested. "Then I will be cold."

Again I heard, "Give him your shirt."

"Lord, it is cold out here," I said. "If I give him my shirt, I
might become sick. Remember that I have to preach tomorrow
night in another city. I cannot do this."

For a third time, I felt the strong impression, "Give him
your shirt."

Without saying a word to the young man, I slowly pulled
my shirt off, slipped it over his head, and drew it down to
cover his chest and back.

He immediately fell on his knees and shouted, "I want to
give my life to Christ."

The film, the sermon, nor the painting was what moved
him. Through an act of love he finally heard the message of
Christ.

Paul said, "For [if we are] in Christ Jesus, neither circum-
cision nor uncircumcision counts for anything, but only faith
activated and energized and expressed and working through
love" (Gal. 5:6, *The Amplified Bible*).

Words are not enough to reach our needy world. Accompany words with action—the action of love. I learned this by

hearing the Holy Spirit speaking directly to my mind and heart.

The Diamonds of Botswana

While Barbara and I were in the African nation of Botswana, God used diamonds to teach me another important lesson. While these tough and brilliant gems have made this a very wealthy country, I did not see any of them while we were visiting there. Why? All of the raw diamonds are under the ground. I was walking on the surface.

The same thing occurs with the Word of God. Many people will read the Bible briefly, then declare that they don't see anything in it—that it is boring to read. People will say that it makes no sense to them—that it doesn't relate to real life.

What is the problem?

This person is just walking on the surface of God's Word.

Only when you go deep and search for spiritual truths will you discover the Bible's diamonds. These will be mined as you learn to listen to God. Each one is hidden and unique. Take time to hear what the Holy Spirit is saying. He will reveal them to you.

Learning to hear God's voice speak directly to you is the third secret of living under the lordship of Christ.

EIGHTEEN

A Captive Audience

God created human beings for relationship with Him, which is, as we have discussed, accomplished by our surrender to Him. He also has a purpose for our lives in service to Him. He has gifted us and has a specific call for each one of us.

As a high-school student, when I answered God's call to preach the gospel, I thought I was willing to be used of God anywhere, at any time, and in any way. The reality of what that means was driven home in a place and before an audience I could not have imagined.

Inside the jail, a depressed and lonely man waited in fear. Outside, two teenage boys rode through the small, paper-mill town of Bastrop, Louisiana.

As our car passed the local jail, a new group of prisoners was being escorted inside. Seeing this, my friend, Arthur, immediately stopped the car. "Wade," he said, "Let's go inside and preach to those prisoners."

This stunned me. I was only 16 and had never been inside a jail. My response was, "No. I will preach at First Baptist Church but not in a jail."

Undeterred, my friend stepped out of the car and said enthusiastically, "Let's go."

He was already across the street when I reluctantly got out and followed him. As I approached, he was asking the jailers if we could go inside and preach the gospel to all the prisoners.

"Sure," they responded. "Go ahead."

Stepping inside of a jail for the first time in my life, I was frightened to death. I followed my bold friend as closely as possible as we climbed the stairs to where the prisoners were held behind bars. When my friend started speaking, I stood behind him.

He introduced himself and me and said, "Men, we aren't here to judge you. We are here because of love. We want to share the love of God with you today."

In amazement, I watched prisoners stop what they were doing and begin to listen. My friend preached his heart out. He concluded by asking those who would like to repent and give their lives to Christ to step to the bars, kneel on the floor, and pray with him.

Slowly, several men stepped forward and knelt. Some of them wept. The Holy Spirit had completely taken over the jail. I witnessed something I had never seen before.

When that impromptu service was over, I was shaken and ready to leave as soon as possible. A big lump of fear was still stuck in my throat, but God wasn't through in that place.

As we left, a jailer said, "Boys, we have another cell in the back. Would you like to go back there and preach?"

With no hesitancy, my bright-eyed friend, Arthur, said, "Yes."

All I could do was follow the jailer into the back section of the jail. As we walked, Arthur said, "Wade, this time you are going to do the preaching."

"Oh, no," I protested. "You are doing just great."

"Oh, yes," he insisted. "This time you are going to preach."

Although I knew God had called me to preach, I had no experience preaching. I had imagined preaching to people inside a church building. Now, I was faced with the fact that my first sermon was going to be in a jail. I had no idea what to do.

At the time, two men—Billy Graham and Billy Sunday— symbolized for me what preaching was all about. I had seen the television coverage of Billy Graham preaching dramatically to 100,000 people in the Los Angles Coliseum. I had read a book about how Billy Sunday, a former baseball player, used big, dynamic gestures to make his points. I thought, "I'll just do what they did."

As I began my sermon that day in the jail cell, I opened the little, red, pocket New Testament my dad had given me. I read from it and clutched it in my hand as I preached. I can't remember much about the message, but I remember talking loud, making big sweeping gestures with my hands, and kicking up my feet just like I envisioned the great Billy Sunday doing. I preached as though thousands of people were in front of me, while in reality, I stared into the eyes of only one, elderly prisoner. By the time I finished, he may have been more afraid than I was.

Finally, I asked him if he would like to give his heart to Jesus. He said, "Yes."

He prayed, surrendering his life to Christ. We rejoiced.

As we walked out, the jailer said, "Boys, let me tell you about that man. He has been found guilty of a serious crime and sentenced to die in the electric chair."

This man to whom I had just witnessed and who submitted his life to Christ was going to be strapped in the electric chair at Louisiana's state penitentiary in Angola. He was on his way to "The Chair!" He was going to die.

As this soaked in, God spoke to me in a way that totally changed my life. He said, "That man had no way to go to church. If he was going to hear the gospel, the church had to go to him. I want you to spend your life taking the gospel to where people are, outside the walls of church buildings."

Since that day, taking the gospel to where people are has been the passion of my life and the essence of my ministry.

For the next nine years, until I finished seminary and went to the international mission field, I continued to preach in that jail and in others. I can honestly say that while visiting jails, I learned how to preach.

What a school that was! I could preach as long as I wanted. No matter how bad the sermon was, no one was going to leave. My audience was literally captive. My vision and my training were grounded in the most unlikely place—a jailhouse in a small, paper-mill town in north Louisiana.

In that practical school, I learned that getting your vision from God and walking in obedience to that vision is vital. This must be done even if you are called to do it in a small, unknown, and unlikely place.

In such a place, real ministry began for me, but it occurred as a result of an earlier decision—to surrender my life totally 24 hours a day, seven days a week to the lordship of Jesus Christ. When I made that lordship commitment to Him, my life was radically changed.

Serving Christ does not require a dynamic experience as I just described. Serving others that they may also know Christ will be a natural outgrowth of surrendering one's life to Christ.

God has a purpose to accomplish in and through you. His strategy (plan) for your life is realizing that purpose begins with your complete surrender to Him. That surrender may take you into places and situations you can't picture now, but you will go with His presence and in His power.

As God uses you in His service, He wants your life to be a witness to Him as He desires to use you to bring others to know Him as Lord.

NINETEEN

Extraordinary Encounters

A businessman and I had gone to a busy steak house for lunch. Before we ate, we went into the men's room to wash our hands. When my companion left, I thought I was alone. Then I realized that someone was in one of the stalls. I felt the Holy Spirit saying, "Wade, witness to that man."

"I can't even see him," I argued.

Again, I was prompted, "Wade, witness to that man."

"Lord," I asked, "How can I witness to someone who can't see me?"

For a third time, I felt God telling me, "Witness to the man inside that stall."

Not wanting to disobey God, I cleared my throat and said, "Sir, may I ask you a spiritual question?"

"Yes," a voice replied.

This time, I asked, "If you die tonight, do you know for sure that you will go to Heaven?"

He said, "No."

With renewed confidence, I asked, "May I share with you how you can be certain that you are going to Heaven?"

He answered, "Yes."

So, with him on one side of the stall door and me on the other, I explained the gospel and told him how to receive Jesus Christ into his life.

Finally, I asked, "Sir, would you like to give your life to Jesus right now?"

Suddenly, the door opened. This stranger fell on his knees in front of me. Earnestly, he said, "Yes, I would."

While I knelt beside him on the floor of that public restroom, he prayed and received Christ into his life.

When I returned to our table, I said nothing about what had just happened. Soon, however, the man from the restroom approached me and said, "Thank you! Thank you!"

Bewildered, my friend at the table asked the man, "What are you thanking him for?"

Happily, this new believer related what had happened in the restroom. Then, he asked us to visit his home. The next day, my companion and I responded to his invitation and had the joy of leading his father to Christ.

A person may tell me that he has had the baptism of the Holy Spirit, that he is Spirit-filled, that he is Christ-controlled, even that he has had a rapturous experience that resulted in a dozen white doves circling his head; but if he cannot listen to God's voice, be obedient and share his faith with lost people, I will tell him that he is not filled with the Holy Spirit. Being filled with God's Spirit will always result in your sharing your faith with people who do not know Christ.

An Appointment in the Desert

In Acts, we learn about Philip, a faithful layperson whom God used powerfully to preach Christ to the Samaritans. However, that evangelistic ministry was interrupted when he was led out of the city and into the desert.

In Acts 8:26, the Bible says, "An angel of the Lord spoke to Philip saying, 'Arise and go south to the road that descends from Jerusalem to Gaza.' (This is a desert road.)"

Philip was taken from preaching to large crowds to share with one man, an Ethiopian. He was sent to witness to the person who may have been the first Gentile convert to Christ. This was a Great Commission breakthrough. The Romans and

Greeks considered Ethiopia to be truly at the "ends of the earth."

Philip was indeed led by the Holy Spirit to the ends of the Palestinian world of his day. Gaza lay about 50 miles southwest of Jerusalem.[1] South and west of there, the desert trailed off into the Sinai Peninsula. From Gaza to Egypt was nothing but barren wilderness. In this isolated place, the evangelist found the object of his mission.

In Acts 8:27-28, the Bible says, "And he arose and went; and there was an Ethiopian eunuch, a court official of Candace, queen of the Ethiopians, who was in charge of all her treasure; and he had come to Jerusalem to worship. And he was returning and sitting in his chariot, and was reading the prophet Isaiah."

Two things are immediately obvious about this man. First, he was a eunuch. Secondly, he was the minister of finance for his country.

In the Old Testament Ethiopia was referred to as the Kingdom of Cush and would have been in Southern Egypt. Its population consisted of black people.[2]

This man would have been a slave as a boy and would have been castrated. In the ancient world, slaves were often castrated in order to be used as keepers of harems and treasuries. They proved to be loyal and trustworthy.

This practice of a eunuch being placed over the treasury was so widespread that, eventually, the name became a synonym for "treasurer." Referring to a guardian of the treasury as a eunuch did not necessarily imply that he had been castrated. However, probably the man to whom Philip was sent was actually a physical eunuch.

This meant that membership in the congregation of Israel was not possible for him. In Deuteronomy 23:1, the law stated, "No one who is emasculated, or has his male organ cut off, shall enter the assembly of the Lord."

As a eunuch, he could visit the temple in Jerusalem, but he could not enter it.[3]

As he traveled back to his home, the Ethiopian read from the scroll of the prophet Isaiah. This Old Testament book offered the great hope for someone in this man's condition. What a promise to an outcast eunuch!

Isaiah 56:3-5 says, "Let not the foreigner who has joined himself to the Lord say, 'The Lord will surely separate me from His people.' Nor let the eunuch say, 'Behold, I am a dry tree.' For thus says the Lord, 'To the eunuchs who keep My sabbaths, and choose what pleases Me, and hold fast My covenant, to them I will give in My house and within My walls a memorial, and a name better than that of sons and daughters; I will give them an everlasting name which will not be cut off.'"

The eunuch must have been startled to look down and see Philip running beside his chariot and listening to what he was reading aloud. He must have thought, "Where in the world did this man arrive from? What is he doing here?"

Philip asked, "Do you understand what you are reading?"

He answered, "Well, how could I, unless someone guides me?"

He needed a Christian interpreter.[4]

Acts 8:31 says, "He invited Philip to come up and sit with him."

Responding to this invitation, Philip climbed into the chariot and seated himself beside the eunuch. He had already heard the man reading from Isaiah 53:7-8, one of the most difficult Old Testament passages to interpret. It depicts the pattern of Christ's suffering, humiliation, and exaltation. Its word picture is of a slaughtered lamb. It evokes the image of Jesus' crucifixion.

John Polhill interprets the heart of verse eight as "His life was taken from the earth."

He concludes that this refers to the glory of His resurrection and His exaltation to the right hand of God.[5]

For Philip, this passage from Isaiah was just a starting point. The Bible says that he "opened his mouth, and beginning from this Scripture he preached Jesus to him" (Acts 8:35).

Amazingly, at a critical point in Philip's sharing, they arrived at a pool of water in the desert. Deeply under conviction and drawn by the Holy Spirit, the eunuch shouted, "Look! Water! What prevents me from being baptized?"[6]

There, in the wilderness, Philip saw the double hindrances of physical and racial prejudice fall away. A eunuch who was a Gentile black man was baptized and received into full membership in the body of Christ.[7] (The Greek word *baptizo* always carries the idea of total submersion.) Two major barriers had been crossed: cultural and racial.

With his mission accomplished, Phillip was led by the Holy Spirit on a preaching mission to northern coastal cities. Rejoicing, the eunuch continued southward. He was the first African convert to Christ.[8]

What God did through Philip in that one day was remarkable. He used Philip to pioneer the missionary effort to the Samaritans. He thus paved the way for the Gentile mission.[9] This is a classic illustration of what can be accomplished when a person is totally surrendered to Christ and obedient to the Holy Spirit's leadership. God's sovereign power was demonstrated even though it meant Philip leaving the crowds and going to share his faith with just one man who religious society considered as an outcast and unworthy of God's love and salvation.

Parking-Lot Evangelism

One night, after midnight, I drove down a dark and lonely Louisiana highway. Glancing to my right, my attention was drawn to one car in the dirt parking lot of a nightclub. I could see a man and woman hugging and kissing inside the car. Clearly, the Holy Spirit said, "Wade, go back and witness to that couple."

Not wanting to hear that, I stepped on the accelerator and sped away. As I did so, I heard the prompting of the Spirit again: "Wade, go back and witness to that couple."

Instead, I drove even faster.

Well, as you have already learned, more than one time is usually necessary to really get my attention. Sure enough, for a third time, I knew that God was saying, "Wade, go back and witness to that couple."

Knowing the foolishness of disobeying God, I slowed the car, turned around, and drove back to that nightclub. When I parked beside the couple, they were not even aware of my presence.

With much trepidation, I knocked on their side window. Startled, the man looked up, rolled down his window, and asked in a tough voice, "What do you want?"

Trusting God for boldness, I asked, "Sir, if you die tonight, do you know if you will go to Heaven?"

For a moment, he looked completely baffled, then in a milder voice he responded, "No, but would you get inside this car and tell me about it?"

An encounter such as this was beyond me. God had arranged it. I simply had the joy of seeing Him at work in an unusual situation.

Surrendering to the lordship of Christ will result in your being filled with the Holy Spirit and having His power in witnessing and ministering to those in need.

Not all witnessing experiences are as dramatic as the ones I've described. Every ministry encounter is in the providence of God and does share the common factor of simply sharing Christ in God's power and leaving the results to Him. Yet exactly how do you go about that ministry so that you will be effective?

---

[1]Kenneth O. Gangel, *Holman New Testament Commentary: Acts* (Nashville: Broadman and Holman, 1998), 125.

[2] John Polhill, *The New American Commentary, Acts* (Nashville,: Broadman and Holman, 1992, 223.

[3]Ibid., 223-224.

[4]Ibid., 224.

[5]Ibid.

[6]Acts 8:36.

[7]Pohill, 225.

[8]Polhill, 226.

[9]Pohill, 226-228.

TWENTY

Love Without Borders

True ministry and service are all about showing God's love in practical ways. The Apostle Paul indicated that the only thing that really counts is love.[1]

Jesus said, "A new commandment I give to you, that you love one another, even as I have loved you, that you also love one another. By this all men will know that you are My disciples, if you have love for one another" (John 13:34-35).

Sometimes this is a call to love the unlovely.

The Little Rock

She was a little street child. Life had dealt harshly with her. She was dirty and alone. Most of all, she was hungry.

Slowly, she walked down the sidewalk in front of a self-serve buffet restaurant. She watched people as they stacked food on their plates.

Suddenly, out of anger and frustration, she picked up a rock and threw it into the restaurant. The rock hit a customer on the head.

Mauricio, the owner, ran outside, grabbed her, picked her up, and shook her. He intended to teach her a good lesson in proper behavior and manners.

Out of nowhere, a woman appeared on the scene. She looked Mauricio in the eyes and said, in Portuguese, "*Não é assim. Não é assim.*" ("That is not the way. That is not the way.")

When she spoke those words, the Holy Spirit spoke to Mauricio's heart regarding helping the eight-million street children of Brazil. This one incident changed his life.

He began opening his restaurant after hours in order to feed the street children. He got to know them and played soccer with them in the evenings. They began to talk to him about needing a safe place to stay.

Mauricio and his wife, Alessandra, are not wealthy, but they felt led to step out by faith and rent a little house for the boys who live on the streets of Contagem, Minas Gerais, Brazil.

At this point, my wife, Barbara, became involved in the story. She has a master's degree in social work from the University of Texas and is a missionary involved in developing human-needs ministries. Her spiritual gift is mercy. She has a compassionate heart for people who suffer and hurt. God's allowing her to become involved with Mauricio and his ministry to street children was not a surprise, spiritually speaking.

As things developed, Barbara was led to share the vision of helping the children of Contagem with two of our closest friends in the United States—Gary Taylor, owner of Gary Taylor Investments, and Phil Jett, pastor of Englewood Baptist Church, both in Jackson, Tennessee. They agreed to go to Brazil with a volunteer team and build a two-story home for these street kids. Miraculously, the home was built in eight days.

In five years, Mauricio's burden resulted in a two-story home for the street boys; a bakery vocational-training school; a chapel for the community; a day-care center, which works with more than 130 children each day; a primary school for more than 230 children, who are the poorest of the poor; a dental and medical facility; a computer school; a vocational-training program to teach teen-agers to be office workers;

health-care classes, and a ministry that touches more than 1,000 children each day.

All of this has grown from a little rock thrown by an angry and hungry little girl. Jesus said that His Kingdom would grow like a mustard seed. We are told to think big, but God wants us to take little steps of faith. Eventually, over time, these will lead to big things. That is the way of Jesus.

It all begins when someone surrenders his life totally to Christ as Lord, hears His voice speak, receives a small vision, takes the first step of obedience by faith, and goes on walking, one step at a time.

Loving God's Way

Beginning with his encounter with that rock-throwing street child, Mauricio learned something we all can learn, if we are to make a difference in our world. He discovered the difficult reality of loving as Jesus loves us.

If you are to obey your Lord's command in John 13:34-35, first understand how He loves you.

During our Pioneer Evangelism Conferences around the world, Barbara shares many of her human-needs ministry experiences. She always stresses that basically two kinds of real love exist—unconditional and sacrificial.

God's love for us is unconditional. It does not depend on us. Who we are, where we were born, or what we do are not important. He loves us, whether we love Him or hate Him.

You may choose to follow Jesus or to go your own way. God still loves you.

Jesus is our example for unconditional love. When He chose His disciples, He called Matthew, a tax collector.[2] This man was hated. People deeply resented what he did. They angrily called him a sinner.

In spite of this, Jesus loved him. He saw a man who was hurting, rejected, and lost. Matthew was a man for whom

Jesus was willing to die. He extended friendship to him and invited him to be one of His disciples.

Like Matthew, we can be thankful that Jesus' love does not depend on our merit. He commands us to love in the same way.

God commands, "You shall love your neighbor as yourself" (Lev. 12:?). One day Jesus called this to the attention of a lawyer who was challenging him. The man returned with the question, "And who is my neighbor?"[3]

Jesus answered with a parable. He demonstrated that the man's neighbors included those against whom he was most prejudiced—the Samaritans.[4]

As followers of Jesus, we have no choice about whom we love. He has made it clear. We are to love all people of all classes and castes, be they friend or foe, rich or poor, clean or dirty.

God is love.[5] His greatest expression of love was the cross. He still wants to show the world His love. How? He wants to do it through you.

Will you allow God to love through you? Will you reach out unconditionally to people who are lost and hurting? Will you show God's love to them in practical ways?

Jesus is also our example for sacrificial love. When He was told about the death of John the Baptist, the Bible says, "He withdrew from there in a boat, to a lonely place by Himself; and when the multitudes heard of this, they followed Him on foot from the cities. When He went ashore, He saw a great multitude, and felt compassion for them and healed their sick" (Matt. 14:13-14).

Even though Jesus wanted some time away from the crowds, He was always ready and willing to help those who approached Him. He always gave of Himself to people who cried out in real need. He gave them His time and energy. With great compassion, He touched the lost and hurting. He never told anyone, "I'm too busy to help you."

Loving does not require money. It does require time and energy.

In Galatians 6:2, we are told to "bear one another's burdens."

When someone is hurting or in need, walking with him or her through pain and crisis takes a lot of your emotional energy. Often, that person will require months or years to recover. Be willing to continue standing with him or her.

Are you willing to give up your time to invest it in another life? Are you willing to sacrifice your life to show God's love?

Jesus commands us to love as God loves, unconditionally and sacrificially. He said, "By this all men will know that you are My disciples, if you have love for one another" (John 13:35).

If you consistently show God's love unconditionally and sacrificially, people will see His love in you. They will know that you are different and will want to understand why. The love of God will open their hearts to hear and receive the good news about Jesus.

When the world gives you something, it wants something in return. When you demonstrate the love of God, ask for nothing in return.

Stop right now. Reflect on what you have just read. Ask yourself, "How can I show God's love in practical ways? How can I serve my community in the name of Christ? How can my church go into our community and show God's love?"

From the Killing Fields to Christ

In Cambodia, Barbara and I visited the Tuol Sleng prison and the "Killing Fields." We were trying to comprehend what the people of this Southeastern Asia country had endured.

For many years, the Cambodians suffered under the cruel Khmer Rouge regime of the dictator, Pol Pot. The Tuol Sleng was the secret enforcement arm of this tyrannical government.

Its prison formerly had been the Tuol Svay Prey High School. Four buildings housed the administration offices, interrogation rooms, and torture chambers. More than 10,000 people, from all parts of the country, were tortured and executed in this place of horror. These included those from every walk of life: farmers, engineers, technicians, professors, government ministers, and diplomats. Entire families, including babies, died in this place.

As we walked through the bloodied ground that had earned the name of the "Killing Fields", we grappled with the realization that Pol Pot had emptied the entire capitol city of Phnom Penh and forced everyone into the countryside. He then ordered thousands of people to be executed and buried in mass graves under the ground on which we were standing. Today, human skulls still can be found there.

Later, we had the honor of worshiping in a small village church. The pastor, whom I will call Mr. C, at age 6 was taken from his home and parents. For four years, he spent his childhood in a labor camp. Day after day, he lifted heavy baskets of cow manure to his head and carried them across rice fields.

When he was 10, Pol Pot's regime fell. The child was free to return home. While he walked back to Phnom Penh, searching for his old house, Mr. C miraculously met his mother on the same road. She had also been released from her prison. His father had died in another camp.

Years later, Mr. C's wife met a man who had returned to Cambodia after going to the United States of America as a refugee. He shared with her the good news about Jesus. She opened her heart, accepted Christ into her life, and began following Him.

Mr. C was not so quick to accept this foreign religion, but eventually he began visiting a Christian preaching point. Drawn by the Holy Spirit, he also trusted Jesus as his Lord and Savior.

For some time, the pastor, who was preaching in that place, had been praying for God to raise up a local leader. As he discipled Mr. C, his prayers were answered. He saw his new convert grow, answer the call to preach the gospel, and assume the leadership of the church.

God gave Mr. C a burden for Muslims in a neighboring village, but they would not allow him to share Jesus there. Finally, he was led to ask the Muslim leader for permission to teach his people to read. While he was not willing for the Christian preacher to enter his village, he did agree for some of the people to go to another location for reading classes.

As this work continued successfully, the leader began trusting and respecting Mr. C. At last, he was invited to visit the village for his teaching.

One day, Mr. C and another Christian missionary visited the village's mosque. The Muslim leader told his people, "These men know more about God than I do."

Then, he asked the preachers of the gospel to teach his congregation!

Can you imagine that? For a long time, God's love had been quietly shown through His messenger, who was patiently teaching the villagers to read. This service, which asked nothing in return, opened the heart of a Muslim leader. Christ was preached in a mosque!

God's love, shown God's way, has the power to open the most closed heart.

Ask God to fill you with His unconditional love and give you a sacrificial heart to reach out and touch lost people in His name. This is the natural outgrowth of a life that is totally surrendered to Christ's control.

[1] 1 Corinthians 13 and Galatians 5:6.
[2] Matthew 9:9-13.
[3] Luke 10:29.
[4] Luke 10:30-37.
[5] 1 John 4:16.

TWENTY-ONE

Amazing Grace

For years, I heard grace explained as "God's Riches At Christ's Expense." I had defined it as God's undeserved favor. However, my good friend, Bill Elliff, senior pastor of the Summit Church in Little Rock, Arkansas, goes further. He rightfully teaches that grace is something God daily gives us. Through this grace He enables us to live. It is the power to obey God when you do not have the desire to do so. It is God's strength when you really desire to obey Him, but you do not have the strength in yourself to do so.

Bill points out that only one way exists to obtain the grace of God in your daily life. You must be willing to humble yourself before Him.

You may ask, "What does that mean?"

It means that you must arrive at the point where you can admit that you have sinned and that you need God's help. Until then, you will live in pride. Not even God can help you.

Whenever you confess your sin and your need, you will receive God's grace and power to deal with the issues of life. No humility equals no grace. It is your decision. Decide if you want to live with or without God's daily grace.

When you decide to surrender your life to Christ as Lord, it is not an act of self-effort. It is an act of grace on God's part. He sends the Holy Spirit to show you your need. He gives you the power to make the right decision. Yes, you must exercise your own free will, but even that is a grace gift.

The Bible speaks of three types of grace. First, we examine saving grace.

Mr. Q

Mr. Q was born in the interior of Vietnam, about 20 miles northeast of Hanoi. When he was 14, wanting to be a soldier, he joined the North Vietnamese Army. For four years, he served as a carrier of information and letters to a military school that trained pilots. In 1951, the army sent him to China for two years for training in the operation of anti-aircraft guns. In 1953, he returned to Vietnam in time to see action in the wars against the French and the Americans. In 1973, he joined the Communist Party.

When he was 62, Mr. Q heard the gospel for the first time. His niece presented it to him. He did not easily accept this as truth. First, he thoughtfully read the entire Bible. When he saw what was said about the end times, he realized how many of these things were being fulfilled in his lifetime. He was filled with fear about what would happen to him at death. This led to his committing his life to Jesus as Lord.

As a new believer, such biblical passages as Matthew 24, Mark 13, and the Revelation strengthened him.

One of the secretaries of the Communist Party told Mr. Q that Christianity was also a party and that he could not be both a Communist and a Christian. He immediately wrote a letter to party officials, asking permission to leave the Communist Party. He declared that he was now a follower of Christ. In the letter, he quoted many Scriptures.

This resulted in him and his family suffering persecution. When a family member sought employment with the government or applied for admission to a government school, the process was very difficult. Some members of the Communist Party, who had been friends, now hated him. Other people observed what was happening to him and his family and wanted to understand why he was willing to endure this. Of course, this gave him many opportunities to witness for Christ.

Mr. Q began a church in his home He was the leader of the church. Local officials responded to this by warning all 29 church members that they were not to attend any kind of religious meeting at Mr.Q's home.

Knowing that Vietnamese leaders had officially declared that people were free to follow whatever religion they chose, Mr. Q wrote another letter. This time, he asked government superiors to rebuke those under them for not allowing the free expression of religion.

Instead of responding to his letter, the local authorities took Mr. Q's Bible and guitar. He told them that they would be punished for touching God's property. Saying that he did not want them to experience God's punishment, he asked them to return the property.

Mr. Q's life story is a perfect picture of God's saving grace. If God can so transform the life of a man who was formerly committed to the Communist Party and its principles, He can do the same for you.

In Ephesians 2:8-9, the Bible reminds you that "by grace you have been saved through faith; and that not of yourselves, it is the gift of God; not as a result of works, so that no one should boast."

The Trash Dump

God not only supplies saving grace, He gives living grace. This is His granting of strength and wisdom to cope with the everyday issues of life. Sometimes, before we can receive and experience living grace, we must be broken. God has to get our attention before He can bless us and move us forward.

My friend, Danny Akin, president of Southeastern Baptist Theological Seminary, has given me permission to share his testimony regarding living grace.

In 1985, Danny resigned from his position on a church staff because he disagreed with the pastor over moral and ethical behavior. He recalls that he was so naive that he didn't know that by resigning, he would lose all of his insurance benefits.

He faced a major crisis. He and his wife had three children. A fourth was on the way. Although he had earned his bachelor's and master's degrees and was working on his doctorate, these could not put bread on his table. He had to quickly find a way to pay bills and feed his family. In Dallas he took a menial job that paid $5.50 per hour. Finding himself in this position did little to boost his self-esteem, he recalls.

In July, 1985, the owner of the real-estate office where he worked approached Danny. Looking sheepish, the owner said, "Danny, I hate to ask you to do this, but we have a problem with one of the shopping centers that we are building up in McKinney. We have a dumpster in the back where the construction guys have been putting their garbage. They filled it up and started dumping stuff on the ground around it. The mess got to be so great that the garbage-collection people couldn't even get to the dumpster to empty it. They responded by bringing a second dumpster and placing it next to the old one. Now, they are telling us that the old one is so full that they can't empty it. Too much trash is on the ground around the new one. I need for you to go up there and get all the garbage off the ground and put it into the empty dumpster. Then you need to climb into the full dumpster and move some of its contents into the new one, so that the loads are evened out. Once you get this done, the company will empty both dumpsters. Hopefully, we won't have this problem again."

So Danny found himself, in 105-degree Texas heat, standing in garbage. He threw the mess from one dumpster into another. He then started gathering trash from the parking lot and dumping it.

He says, "To be perfectly transparent with you, the whole thing ticked me off with God. I said, 'You are the Lord of the universe, but in this particular case, I'm convinced that You have no idea what You are doing.'"

He said, "I explained to God that I had bachelor's and master's degrees from Southwestern Baptist Theological Seminary. I reminded Him that I graduated with a 3.53 grade average. I brought up that I was working on a Ph.D at the University of Texas in Arlington. I included that I had preached in some really nice churches and for some years had been told that I was a pretty good preacher. I said, 'God, it just seems to me that this is a huge waste of my talent and ability. I could be put to better service for the Kingdom than to be throwing garbage from one dumpster to another.'"

At lunchtime, his frustration was mollified briefly when one of the Dallas real-estate agents drove to McKinney to buy him a good meal. By early afternoon, however, he was back in the dumpster—griping, complaining, and arguing with God.

Finally, he sensed the Lord asking, "Danny, what if it is My will for you to be in this dumpster right now? Would you really want to be somewhere else?"

He did not answer that question immediately because his reaction would have been to say, "Yes, I'd rather be some-where else. This is just lunacy."

God gave Danny enough wisdom for him to stew over the question before answering. After a long time, Danny spoke to the Lord, "I don't understand. I did the right thing. I acted with moral purity and integrity when I resigned from the church. You know that I did. Yet, here I am in this garbage. What am I doing in this?"

Then Danny added, "I don't understand it, but yes, I'd much rather be in Your will in a dumpster than to be anywhere else in the whole wide world."

Ten years later, almost to the month, Danny had the joy of standing in the Georgia Dome in Atlanta and preaching during the Pastor's Conference at the Southern Baptist Convention. Thousands of pastors from across the nation heard him that day.

In 1992, God moved Danny to Southeastern Baptist Theological Seminary, where he became a professor of theology and the dean of students. In 1996, he was called to Southern Baptist Theological Seminary, where he was promoted to the prestigious position of vice-president for academic administration and the dean of theology. Then in 2003 he was elected to return to Southeastern and serve as president of that seminary.

Danny testifies to God's living grace. He says that the God who has put him where he is today can put him right back in a dumpster tomorrow. The issue is not where he wants to go but where God wants him to be.

Danny says, "I really don't want to go through it again, but having been there and having seen what God did, I know that I would not be where I am today if He had not taken me through those experiences."

He adds, "Yes, I can say, 'If it is Your will to put me in a dumpster again, then do it.'"

No place is better than being in the center of God's will and having His purpose fulfilled for your life. This is true even when things don't make sense—when you don't understand why you are where you are, doing what you are doing.

God's grace put Danny Akin in that dumpster because He knew exactly how He wanted to prepare him for life and ministry. Sure, he had been to school, but God had one more special school for him—the School of Living Grace (2 Cor. 12:9).

Facing the Shot

In 1967, Lt. William Calley took his platoon into My Lai, a little village in Quang Nai province in the northern part of South Vietnam. A slaughter that spared no one ensued. The front cover of *Life* carried photos of this massacre of men, women, children, and babies. Many people believe that this grisly incident was the turning point in the Vietnam conflict.

Once its details were publicized, homefront resistance to America's involvement in the war flared to new heights.

In the aftermath of the My Lai massacre occurred a brief story that intersected my life with that era of history.

About 1,000 people from the My Lai area were transferred to the Central Vietnam coastal jungle area near Cam Ranh Bay. Southern Baptists had a missionary couple, Walter and Pauline Routh, stationed there. Some people believe that Walter is the best missionary ever to set foot in Southeast Asia. By God's grace, I was assigned to work with him.

Walter and Pauline lived in the village of Ba Ngoi, just five miles north of Cam Ranh Bay. I lived about two hours up the road in Nha Trang. This put us near the new refugee settlement, which they called My Cã.

Walter felt God's leading to begin a work in this refugee settlement. To get to it, a person had to travel five miles into the jungle on a dirt road off Vietnam's main north/south highway. My mentor, Walter, and I made the journey together. Walter took a generator into the new village, showed a movie about Jesus Christ, taught the Bible, led many people to faith in Christ, and started a new church. Weekly I went in to work with and minister to the young people.

We worked together in this project until one night when Walter had to make an unexpected trip to Saigon. This meant that I was left to make the trip through the jungle to My Cã alone. As I turned off the main highway and onto the dirt road that led to the settlement, bright yellow flares began falling from the sky.

These flares lit up the area toward which I was driving my Volkswagen van. Clearly some sort of activity was occurring in the jungle near My Cã. Although I was apprehensive, I continued on the road into the jungle.

I continued driving down the road but soon noticed in the darkness the outline of a large log lying across the road. I realized that the roadblock was intentional; my first thought was, "I am in serious trouble."

Then I saw the soldiers standing up from behind the log with AK rifles pointed directly at me.

As I pressed myself down onto the front seat and waited, three thoughts flashed through my mind: I am going to die, right here and now; I will never ever see my mom again; Am I sure that I am saved?

A peace flooded my heart, confirming that I was saved and ready to die. In that quiet moment of assurance, I realized that the shooting had stopped just as fast as it had started.

Still gripped by fear, I crawled out of the van, knelt in the middle of the road, and lifted my hands over my head. As a captain walked toward me, I knew that I faced five possibilities. The first possibility was that these were North Vietnamese soldiers. If they were, I would be headed to the prison in Hanoi. Secondly, they could be Viet Cong. In this case, I would either be shot immediately, or I would spend the rest of my days in the jungle as their prisoner. The third possibility that these were South Vietnamese or Korean soldiers. If so, they would free me. I could also hope that these were Americans. This would have thrilled me.

When the captain placed the tip of his AK on my nose, I looked directly into his eyes and went weak with relief. Korean!

When I asked if he spoke Vietnamese, he shook his head, indicating that he did not. Neither did he speak English. Then, I saw a cross hanging from a chain around his neck. Quickly, I imitated the Catholics and made the sign of the cross. He smiled and returned the sign, indicating, "Me, too".

We were two believers on a jungle road in the midst of a war zone, being drawn together by the cross.

With signs and broken English, he made me understand that hundreds of soldiers hid in the jungle around me, waiting to launch an attack on communist forces. I had driven into the middle of what was about to explode into a violent battle.

Insisting that all of their shots had been aimed above my van, the captain assured me that they had never intended to kill me. Wanting to confirm this, he accompanied me on an inspection of the mission vehicle.

What happened then caused all of the strength to leave my legs. Just as I entered the van, the windshield was pierced and shattered by a single shot from a 45-caliber pistol. While most of the soldiers shot into the air, one of them had used his side arm to take direct aim at me. Unobstructed, the bullet would have hit me in the heart. Instead, it struck the top of the steering wheel, skimmed down, and slammed into the floorboard at my feet. I had missed death by less than one inch.

God sent his angels to protect me that night. That one shot could have ended my life on that jungle road in May 1968. I would have been catapulted into eternity; everything would have changed. I would have had no wife, no children, no ministry in Washington, no ministry in Brazil, no global ministry, and no grandkids. All that I have done and experienced since then would have been aborted.

Suppose that had happened. Suppose that I had died in Vietnam that night. Then, what?

For any of us, our time to live on Earth is short. Soon, it is all done. Our earthly lives end. Every opportunity and experience on this planet is immediately in the past. The day is coming when you will "face the shot"; your physical life will end. Then, what?

We do not know much about Heaven, but we are certain of one thing: Jesus is there. When I think of this life's dangers and uncertainties, I am encouraged by the realization of His abiding presence and the promise of eternity with Him.

A song that I learned when I was a high-school student returns to me when the challenges of this life seem most threatening. It says, "His word shall not fail you—He promised; Believe Him, and all will be well; Then go to a world that is dying, His perfect salvation to tell! Turn your eyes upon Jesus; Look full in His wonderful face; And the things of earth will grow strangely dim in the Light of His glory and grace."

When the time arrives for you to "face the shot", knowing Him in a vital personal relationship is more than enough. In that moment, nothing else really counts. His dying grace is sufficient.

This has been a story of how, by God's grace, He has done His work in and through me and in the lives of many others as we have chosen to live surrendered to the lordship of Christ. I began this book by asking you to consider the question, "Does my life have significance and purpose? Am I making any significant difference?"

In His Word, God promises that He has a purpose for each one of us. But only by God's grace does He fulfill His purpose to save us and empower us by His Holy Spirit to overcome every struggle and to grow in Him through the painful process of brokenness. By the process of surrendering to His lordship, God molds us, as the potter molds the clay, to accomplish His purpose in our lives and through our lives in service that will glorify our Lord.

What will you choose? Will you choose to live in your own strength with self on the throne or yield to the lordship of Christ and allow Jesus to be the Master?

"All to Jesus I surrender, All to Him I freely give;
I will ever love and trust Him, In His presence daily live.

"All to Jesus I surrender, Humbly at His feet I bow,
Worldly pleasures all forsaken, Take me, Jesus, take me now.

"All to Jesus I surrender, Make me, Savior, wholly Thine.
Let me feel the Holy Spirit, Truly know that Thou art mine.

"All to Jesus I surrender, Lord, I give myself to Thee;
Fill me with Thy love and power, Let Thy blessing fall on me.

"I surrender all, I surrender all,
All to Thee, my blessed Savior, I surrender all."[1]

[1] Words to the hymn "I Surrender All" by J.W. Van De Venter, Public Domain.

How to order more copies of

The 24/7 Christian

and obtain a free Hannibal Books catalog
FAX: 1-972-487-7960
Call: 1-800-747-0738 (in Texas, 1-972-487-5710)
Email: hannibalbooks@earthlink.net
Mail copy of form below to:
Hannibal Books
P.O. Box 461592
Garland, Texas 75046
Visit: www.hannibalbooks.com

Number of copies desired   _____
Multiply number of copies by $9.95   ___X____$9.95___
           Cost of books: $_____

Please add $3 for postage and handling for first book and add
50-cents for each additional book in the order.
          Shipping $_____
   Texas residents add 8.25 % sales tax $_____

          Total order $_____

Mark method of payment:
check enclosed _____
Credit card# _____ exp. date_____
   (Visa, MasterCard, Discover, American Express accepted)

Name _____
Address _____
City State, Zip _____
Phone _____ FAX _____
Email _____

You"ll enjoy these books also

Rescue by Jean Phillips. American missionaries Jean Phillips and husband Gene lived through some of the most harrowing moments in African history of the last half century. Abducted and threatened with death, Jean and Gene draw on God's lessons of a lifetime.

_____Copies at $12.95=_____

Unmoveable Witness by Marion Corley. An alarming interrogation by Colombia's version of the FBI. A dangerous mishap at a construction site. A frightening theft at his home in Bucaramanga, Colombia. What kept Marion and Evelyn Corley on the mission field for 22 years when others might have returned to Stateside comforts?

_____Copies at $9.95=_____

Beyond Surrender by Barbara J. Singerman. A dramatic story of one family's quest to bring light to a dark and desperate world. The Singerman family serves in Benin, West Africa. They confront spiritual warfare beyond anything they expect when they surrender to missions.

_____Copies at $12.95=_____

The Jungle series, also known as the Rani Adventures by Ron Snell. With hilarity, warmth, and spine-tingling suspense, "the Rani Series" trilogy takes readers into the cross-cultural upbringing of Ron Snell, who, with his family, sets aside American comforts to bring the good news of Christ to people in darkness in the Amazon jungles of Peru.

It's a Jungle Out There (Book 1) _____ **Copies at $7.95 =** _____
Life is a Jungle (Book 2) _____ **Copies at $7.95 =** _____
Jungle Calls (Book 3) _____ **Copies at $7.95 =** _____

Add $3.00 shipping for first book, plus 50-cents for each additional book.
Shipping & Handling _____
Texas residents add 8.25% sales tax _____
TOTAL ENCLOSED_____

check ____ or credit card # _____ exp. date_____
(Visa, MasterCard, Discover, American Express accepted)

Name _____

Address _____ Phone _____

City _____ State _____ Zip _____

**For postal address, phone number, fax number, email address
and other ways to order from Hannibal Books, see page 173**

TO CONTACT THE AUTHOR WRITE HIM AT

wade.akins@pobox.com

VISIT THE AUTHOR'S WEB SITE:

www.pioneerevangelism.org